# STOP PLAYING

# &

# TRAP CASH

# STOP PLAYING

# &

# TRAP CASH

By Alfred Harvey

Published by

## MIDNIGHT EXPRESS BOOKS

STOP PLAYING & TRAP CASH

ISBN-10: 0990318389
ISBN-13: 978-0-9903183-8-5

Published by
*Midnight Express Books*
P.O. Box 69
Berryville AR 72616
(870) 210-3772
MEBooks1@yahoo.com

# STOP PLAYING

# &

# TRAP CASH

By Alfred Harvey

# Acknowledgements

For my mother Joyce Burkett-Parsons.

Dedicated to my lifelong friend and brother R.I.P. Vincent "Kubbie" Clardy.

First and foremost I would like to thank God for him constantly surrounding me with his angels of life, love, happiness, and business so no matter how many times fall and scrape my knees he invented tough skins so I am ok.

A big example that his angels do truly exist I would like to give the biggest thank you to Tara D. Jefferson-Harvey for her tireless efforts in handling the manuscript and doing her best to see my vision, and also for constantly coming to give me big kisses while I was incarcerated in some of America's worst dungeons!

I would also like to thank my lawyer Kory Matthewson because if it were not for him I would still be in those dungeons.

I would like to thank my beautiful family , in one way or another each had a part in shaping me into the man I am today, and constantly being in my corner between rounds as I went toe to toe with life .R.I.P. Grandpa Jack, and Aunt Billie, mom, and pops, Joyce, and Reginald Parsons Sr., my brothers, and sisters, Jason, Andrew, Jeremy, Terrence, Reginald Parsons Jr., Lorraine, and Anthony Parsons, Wini Harvey, Jeanette Buirkettt, Judy Jones, and many more other family members that I may have left out I love and miss you all!

To my beautiful children Demitrius, Estashea, Aidan, and Chase Harvey Acuna, Ahnaleis, Ocean Harvey, Jalen Kountz, Christian Jefferson, no matter what always follow your passion, and never stop chasing your dreams and always know I love you unconditionally!

I would thank Joy Hammond Nelson for her great work on my final edit.

I can't forget Terry L. Wroten of No Brakes Publishing for constantly checking on me to make sure I was in the lab on my writing grind.

I would like to thank Leonard Neal Jr. (Itchy) and De Andre Ingram from Pomona, CA for their constant encouragement and assisting me with the pre-editing of my manuscript under those extreme conditions we were in away from our families, and turn a negative situation into a positive, what up ya'll!

I would also like to thank my amazing publishing company Midnight Express Books for their job in bringing my book to life, and making my dream a reality and for assisting individuals behind the wall to publish their work; you guys are awesome.

Last but not least, I would like to thank my readers who extended their hand or heart in supporting me; you know who you are and so does God. Thank you so much! I pray the Lord surrounds you with his angels of happiness, and success because of you I am able to continue chasing my dreams.

Love you and thank you all, God Bless!

# INTRODUCTION

Start and run your own business. Be your own boss, easy money making ideas, turnkey opportunities, get rich using these secrets, start ups with minimum or no investment required, succeed buying and selling real estate, no money down and no credit needed, invent patent and produce a million dollar idea, "what the large print giveth, the small print taketh away."

Allow me to be frank, it's all bull s\*\*t!!! Pardon me, but I'm highly upset. There's a market place for small business bull s\*\*t that exists just to take advantage of us people with dreams of succeeding in our own business. I'm sick and tired of these assholes and their inspirational manipulation, media promotions, TV, radio, public appearances, be your own boss seminars and start up lectures with their boxes and packages of dreams do come true for sale, newspapers, magazines, interviews about their best selling "How-to-books" on business start ups. Forbes magazine warned, "Most How-to-books on entrepreneurship aren't worth a dime." I myself have bought hundreds of them, even used one to level out the fridge once, and one to stop my Christmas tree from leaning one year.

You can compare most business start-ups to a marriage. Most of them fail in their first year, and the longer you remain in one that's not working, the worse off you will be. How many people have you seen get married on impulse and it ends with a huge disastrous consequences? Now there are those people who are not even as smart as you are, and maybe can't even come close to the great ideas you have, and still they make it through the fray and succeed at their own start up. Remember, when it comes to a business start up, there are boundaries; rules and details one must follow to minimize risk. I like to make my point easier by using an example of a multi-billion dollar company which has weathered the storm of business since the Great Depression and that's not common at all. General Electric C.E.O. Jack Welch once said to his company "think small" and this holds true. No matter how mighty a corporation is, it should always have the nimbleness of a small start up or risk being out performed by a younger innovator. So, for a C.E.O. to tell his huge conglomerate to think small, individuals like you and me had better be thinking tiny or even micro, "*Honey I Shrunk The Kids*" small.

So before you go throwing your savings, IRAs, kids college funds or equity in your homes away on impulse, just know that Vegas has better odds and you could have saved a lot of valuable time and stress in the long run dropping it all on one hand of Black Jack. Had a lot of fun and even seen Blue Man Group on your way out and took only the profits from doubling your savings and gambled that on your start up. Take it from a guy like me and keep the majority of your savings.

In business I have been cheated, swindled, jacked, defrauded, scammed, and even fell victim to the, "Be Your Own Boss" manipulations that we all have wasted our time and money on. Now allow me to show you a simpler, cheaper, and easier way to set tiny little traps to catch profit. Note: I will bring up words of wisdom and solid techniques you will need to be aware of and remember. Also included "TRAP UNIVERSITY," an extremely valuable section of STOP PLAYING & TRAP CASH gives you a background and a bird's eye view of simple money making opportunities that work!

I give personal secrets and easy inexpensive ways I trap cash putting emphasis on the How's, What's and Why's of How To Buy Cheap Land and use it to your advantage, now or in the future. How to buy houses cheap for little or nothing on "short sale" and to rent out or flip for quick cash. You will learn the Power Of Liens, how to file a lien on property that has been abandoned, how to secure ownership of vehicles, boats and other property that has been abandoned. You will also learn how to buy Government Tax Lien property for pennies, and when the owners default, you become the new owner of the property. In addition, you will learn how to open your own consignment store and trap huge profits. I will teach you how to bid on storage units, why to start a business, one you can start for under $10,000. Some for even $100 today!

TRAPSTAR DEFINED: A Trapstar is anyone who can be just as confident poor as they are rich; a person who makes money by any means. A trendsetter who understands the art of the possible, and the power of persuasion. An agent of influence. A masterful negotiator who is an expert at facilitating the handshake between the buyer and the seller in any business situation. The Long shot most unlikely to succeed, an inner city people's person: classy, shrewd, serious, and humorous. A silent partner, full of swagger, cutthroat, audacious, a masterful gambler, a risk taker, a hustler, an inventor, a teacher as well as a student, family oriented, tactful, the entrepreneur of today and tomorrow.

To make defining a TRAPSTAR easier just look in the mirror, that's a TRAPSTAR!

If you're not a believer, no worries. Read on and you will be. THAT's my promise to you. Now let's STOP PLAYING & TRAP CASH!

# Table of Contents

# CHAPTER 1

Alfred Harvey

## Section 1—Trap Cash? Yes You Can! Why Do It?

Trapping Cash is possible for anyone and the rewards are great. It's something anybody can do. You can be any age, any race, any gender, and any religion. It's something you will see work. It doesn't cost a lot of money. It doesn't take a long time to get started. It's not hard; it's not just for those with the big educations or some exclusive skill. I recommend anyone contemplating venturing into a start up, or small business, to come down a few notches into the tiny micro world of Trapping Cash. It has also been proven as a very effective way to test products, goods, and services local or even viral. Most people have Trapped Cash many times before; they just may not realize it.

The great thing about Trapping Cash is you can turn it off or on as you please, which is not the case if you have your savings invested into a giant start up. Once you're in, there's no turning back. In Trapping Cash, you set the schedule. You are 100% in charge! So, in reality, you are truly your own boss.

With any process, there are a few rules and principles one should expect, but you are in full control. You can start Trapping Cash today and should not expect a reduction in your gross income, loss, or just breaking even your first couple of years in business, like in the case of a gigantic start up.

Trapping Cash is simple, you don't need to complicate the process, and it will only confuse and discourage you from Trapping huge profits. I've seen it so many times, people, (out of excitement), want to run out and buy the best computer, all the research tools, take a class, (bless their hearts), but you don't need all that stuff. Another big one is procrastination. Let's not act as if we're investing our whole life savings here. Think about it like fishing. When you go out fishing, you're relaxed, you make a little preparation, you're in a great mood, you check the weather, you may check different lakes for certain types of fish and where they're biting the most. When you get there you set up, set your poles up, bait your hooks with fancy weights, floats and lures, many kinds of crawlers the fish you're trying to catch tend to love. You cast your line and sit back, read a book or enjoy a cold drink, maybe even a little conversation. You just sit back, relax, and chill: and wait for your fish to bite.

This is the bait, hook, line and sinker effect. I have been successful at it so many times that I've lost count. When you're at the lake, you're not worried about competition, you don't have someone over your shoulder telling you do this or do that; your life savings is not at risk. You are in full control. The best part is you will be Trapping Cash not fish. "Give a man some cash he can buy fish for a day, teach a man to Trap Cash he can buy fish everyday for life."

## Section 2—Simple Results

I'm going shoot straight from the heart. I never read any other books on, "How To Trap Cash. I'm pretty sure there are a few out there somewhere, but I've never seen one. From me you will get my way, my opinions, and a simple set of rules I have learned to get the best results just by following. I know my way works very well and you will too. It isn't intended to be *The* way to Trap Cash. Just my way, coming from a person who, if he doesn't Trap Cash, he doesn't eat, period!

Every day, every week, every month, and every year I really enjoy seeing an average person grasp the concept of Trapping Cash. It changes them and they stay busy constantly checking their Traps or laying new ones. The only credibility I have is street credibility. It doesn't come from any specialized training, fancy degrees, or grade point averages. It comes from a solid history of results. I started Trapping Cash when I was a kid. I was my own success story. Buying and selling everything under the sun, placing ads in any kind of newspapers I could find. My parents even had to get a second phone line in the house because every time the phone rang it was for me. I had Traps laid all over my city. In classified ads, bulletin boards, even at other local businesses. I had Traps laid all around my house, up and down the street and at other people's houses. I understood sometimes it was about location and presentation.

I was the middle of five brothers and while they were in the house stuck in front of the TV, I was on the side of my mother's house buying and selling everything from cars to electronics, appliances to clothes, animals to firewood, and diapers by the bulk, even medical supplies. Yep, even had a great connection on that for a couple of years. I'd be on the side of the house with a cigarette in my mouth, pocket full of cash, a cordless phones in my hand, ringing off the hook and I wasn't even supposed to be smoking. I even had to hire a few people from the neighborhood to assist customers, some adults, even twice my age. Rumor had it I paid more than the paper route. This was Monday through Friday and on the weekends. I didn't just dominate my yard sales; I dominated everyone's. I was everywhere with a dolly, a red wagon, and sometimes even my grandfather's truck, (RIP Grandpa Jack). I would carry it, drag it and even stash it in the bushes and come back for it later. I was a real busybody, all people could do was shake their heads at me. (Private Smile)

Since then, besides teaching people how a true bottom feeder Traps cash, I have bought, sold, merged over 20 small businesses and counting everything from markets, eateries, salons, print shops, clothing stores, automobile body shops, detailing, tire shops, tow trucks for hire, housekeeping services, commercial janitorial services, carpet cleaning, window cleaning and the list goes on. I even owned a pager shop back in the day. When it comes to trapping cash, I have experienced it all. But if you're talking, I'm listening. I'm going give you some seasoned advice and simple procedures for Trapping Cash.

*If I don't Trap cash, I don't eat."*

Alfred Harvey

## Section 3—People Can Overwhelm – Don't Let'em

Too many people will have many different things to say on how to Trap Cash. Too many books, seminars, lectures, and magazines will only end up confusing and discouraging you. Throw all that junk out. Before I threw it all out, I fell victim to every kind of "be your own boss" and start up scam. So, I stopped listening to everyone, and just followed what works. I didn't realize how basic it was! Listening to many people, How To's, What If's, Look Out's, Might Be's, all the horror stories, and downsides. Take for instance dating! If you get too caught up on all the mentioned details, you'd never go on a date. Trapping Cash is like making love; it's fun, it's easy with huge rewards.

We don't mind handling the if's, might's, and maybe's that may come along in the process. Trapping Cash is not only possible; you won't even encounter many problems or obstacles in the Trapping Cash process. Three basic things you need: The Trap, The Bait, and The Desire.

Alfred Harvey

## Section 4—Big Reasons to Trap Cash

Set traps at all times. That's the objective for best results when Trapping Cash.

You would be shocked to see the many different Cash Trapping portfolios people have set up. Most of them are sharing many private smiles at this very moment.

It won't take you long to assemble and polish your very own Traps.

1. SELF CONFIDENCE

You will admire yourself more than others, when you start Trapping Cash. You start feeling great about yourself. It's a new kind of strut and business swagger that will be noticed by family members and your peers. The ego booster admiration you see in people's eyes, will catapult you all the way to where you want to be.

2. IT'S SO MUCH EASIER NOW

Back in the days, we didn't have all the great tools we have today. When I was younger, we were just grasping the household computer era. So it stayed broken in the corner of the room, and there was no windows. We barely had computers in school and cell phones were bigger than your head. So being today that most people are computer literate, there is a super duper advantage when it comes to Trapping Cash. This is the mobile era. Now with all the downloadable programs, apps, software, and not to mention the social networking, what took most people days, weeks and months, now only takes hours, minutes or seconds. Your reach is now global, not local!

## 3.  YOUR QUALITY OF LIFE

Trapping Cash is better than anything I've ever experienced. You will travel and have more time for vacations, socialize with all kinds of interesting business minded people, learn new skills and information. You will influence so many people around you. You will be able to grasp management structure; organization and it will enrich your life. That's enough alone!

## 4.  ORIGINALITY

We are all unique - like our fingerprints. When we have a passion to succeed at something, nothing or no one can stop us. We have all had experiences, ideas, thoughts, and Trapping Cash has a way of molding to our originality. In the end you will succeed in Trapping large profits in what you love doing. It just seems to happen that way.

## 5.  CHANGE

I've seen grandmothers who have been stuck in their ways for years and when they start to Trap Cash, it's like they caught a second wind and all you can do is look at them and think to yourself "That's what's up! You Go Girl." It's like an old person on the dance floor getting their groove on, you can't tell them nothing!

The change will always be positive. Always!!!

## 7. DO YOU!

The biggest reason to Trap Cash is just to be able to do you. The way you want to do it. Anytime you may feel the need to do it. Whatever that may be is nobody's business. Sometimes when you want to do something, may not be the best time for other people, or you just lack the time or money. There's one thing that will change all of that and make it a lot easier and that's *TRAPPING CASH!* It will help you fulfill that promise you have made to yourself and others so many times, "Someday, someday, *Someday* I'm going to do it!"

Everyone can Trap Cash! Through the years, I've found that to be very true. It drives me crazy because it's just so easy. It's a lemonade stand compared to a gigantic start up. Trapping Cash has affected my life so much in ways I have cried and laughed with happiness. Trapping Cash will open your eyes to skills you never knew you had. We all have ideas that we can turn into cash without gambling our whole life savings. Anything is worth a shot and I urge you to really consider giving it a try. Anyone! Couples, single parents, kids, students, veterans, seniors, and ex-convicts. Any type or variety of business people should try. It will only strengthen you and catapult you into a Utopia of profits. "STOP PLAYING AND TRAP THAT CASH!"

Alfred Harvey

## Section 5—More Great Reasons to Trap Cash

1. To make money independently

2. To get a better place to live

3. To get a better car

4. To travel

5. To test your product before starting a start up

6. To inspire others - kids, grandkids, family or friends

7. To learn a lot more about a field

8. To become an expert

9. To set an Example

10. To shop until you drop

11. To have better connections

12. To have more fun and make new friends

13. To mind your own business

14. To test a new idea

15. To save for retirement

16. To be your own boss

17. To be fulfilled

Through Benjamin Franklin's prolific writings, we learn that

"one's true liberty comes from financial freedom".

TRAP CASH TO BE FREE!

## Section 6—Trap Cash Without A Cause

What's the reason you want to Trap Cash? Who cares, you don't need a reason! Trapping Cash will not be a disappointing experience. You can start Trapping Cash anytime without a cause. That's the joy in it! Trap Cash for exercise. Trap Cash to pass the time. Trap Cash on a whim, or off a dare, Trap Cash just to do something. Trap Cash for fun. Trap Cash just to show off. Trap Cash to get even. Trap Cash for revenge. Trap Cash because of a great loss. Trap Cash just to see if you can. Trap Cash for rent, food, or clothes. Trap Cash to see the profitability from a hobby.

Trap Cash to show your craft or skill. Trap Cash to be a millionaire. Trap Cash to save the environment. Trap Cash for the kids. Trap Cash to show your start up will succeed. Trap Cash to inspire. Trap Cash to fly in a helicopter! Trap Cash to get a date. Trap Cash to get laid. Trap Cash for opportunities. Trap Cash to replace "TV Time." Trap Cash to relieve stress or worry. Trap Cash to relax.

I don't care if it's a dollar, TRAP IT! Whatever you do, do not stop Trapping Cash! Trap Cash while you watch TV Trap Cash on the golf course. Trap Cash while you shop. Trap Cash at the kitchen table. Trap Cash while you drive. Are you getting the point? TRAP CASH! I Trap Cash "to get rich" period! If along the way I can see some really cool stuff, well then that's even better. If you want to Trap Cash as well, then hey, we need to do lunch, follow each other on Twitter, and befriend each other on Facebook. Two Trappers are always better than one. Hell, I'd even like for you to meet my parents. My mother makes a mean meatloaf. Your motive in becoming a Cash Trapper is to catch Cash period!

## Section 7—Believe!

The key to Trapping lots of cash is your swagger. You have got to strut! You have to know and believe you are right and not just think it. You have to know this is the right thing to do and that it is necessary. You have to be arrogantly persistent in a demanding manner, confident, conceited and convinced that you have the power to pursue your catch to the finish. Because you do! You are not uncertain when it comes to being an entrepreneur; the results are in. When it comes to Trapping your cash ... You are the entrepreneur! You're on your own. You work for you. You won't fail, and you are not in the least affected by the haters or critic's ridicule. That's exactly what puts the pep in your step, and if there is one thing you need, it's them. Pursue your catch! "Look around the habitable world. How few know their own good? Or knowing it, pursue it?" Benjamin Franklin.

Alfred Harvey

# CHAPTER 2

Alfred Harvey

## Section 1—Just how long will it take to Trap Cash? Hours, days, weeks, months, years?

All of the above is your answer. Some people are looking at Trapping Cash from the outside and not fully understanding or grasping the Trapping Cash way of life. Nobody is going give you anything! You have to get it yourself. Some people tend to think they will get this thought and then, "Boom!" Just sit at the computer and Trap Cash like the old Hungry Hungry Hippo game with the marbles. They think they're just going open their front door and see a bunch of stacks of cash running around. Some caught in Traps and others they have to dash down the street and catch, as if they were chasing the ice cream truck or something. For me, I would enjoy the challenge, because I'm an Agent of Influence who understands the "art of the possible" and the "Power of Persuasion." Have no fear, when you're done reading this book you will have learned some valuable lessons; and will be able to rise to the occasion. With your new knowledge and swag, you will not only be able to Trap Cash, but you will be able to do it with finesse and flamboyance. It's like having the eye of the Tiger. It's okay to be cocky, even if you're being modest and say you're not. Now I'm not tooting my own horn, but I know I can sit at the computer and Trap Cash with no problem. I do it all the time. I get mail, instant messages, updates, and inside tips. I get numerous amounts of very valuable lists and information on everything from buying and selling, even valuable free stuff. I network and trade information on auctions for cars, property, businesses and anything you can imagine from colored pencils to boats being bought, sold and traded. Even ''You come get it, you can have it'' deals. I can check the classifieds in every state in the country. I can Trap Cash in wanted ads, bargain boxes, and lists of any kind. I can check prices anywhere in the world and I'm just a local boy just trying to make a few odd dollars. I can import or export. *I can Trap Cash "outsourcing" other businesses' or consultant's products, goods or services to other businesses or consultant's in need.* I can sell a Cocker Spaniel to a guy in Florida, or a bulldog to a lady in New York. All while sitting with morning breath, in my favorite *Snoopy* pajamas, on my IPad in California, looking at my friends crashed out all over the place from a party the night before, thinking I need to go shower, and brew some coffee. I'm also confident I can walk out my front door and see endless opportunities to Trap Cash. I see opportunities when I see vacant property, residential or commercial, especially if it's been vacant for a long time. I see opportunities in any For Sale sign on property, cars, boats, or even dusty cars along side of people's houses, oil stained driveways, dirty windows, DIRTY ANYTHING. Overgrown grass or trees, any abandoned or deserted property. There are Lien processes that exist that allow you to take over ownership, some within 45 days! I know cars are 30 days. You just have to have a Lien service attempt to contact the owner. If it's on your property, you can charge Lien costs, storage and towing, or you can help a neighbor if the property is abandoned on their property and Trap Cash. Just being aware of the ''short sale" list on houses I was able to buy a house in Arizona for $7,000 and within the same week sold it for $28,000. There are sales like this on everything under the sun. The seller gets a deal as well as the buyer. It's nobody's business what you paid for it. I do it all the time. I had a friend come to me whom I've known since sixth grade and he asked me if I could assist him in learning to Trap Cash because he was doing bad and seen I wasn't. So, being an old friend, we took a ride in my Escalade and I explained that there are a few things he can do today, and after a week or so, he would never have to look back. I was going to prep him the same way I got started and he said a week was too long; he needed money today, but never said it was life or death. He was wasting my time not listening.

I already envisioned the $4,000 he was going to have in his hands. Two weeks later, I got a call from him while I was on a first class flight saying he was in the exact same situation as before. I told him I would call him when I got back in town. I never did. So I ask, "How long is it going take before you1re really serious about trapping cash?" Don't think too long!

Alfred Harvey

## Section 2—Just how much does it cost to trap cash? $100? $1,000? $10,000?

Again all of the above. It is going be easier to trap $1,000 if you already have $1,000, but with Trapping Cash, you can start with absolutely zero. You would be surprised at the allowances agents in the middle of transactions trap. They're called commissions. There's no limit on them in some situations. For example, if you were the one who found that house I bought on short sale for $7,000, I wouldn't have had a problem giving you a significant commission on the quick sale price of $28,000.

Now imagine if you had several Traps set just like that on a non-stop basis among others. You had no out of pocket expense except for the time that it took for both of us to Trap Cash. Imagine that . . . zero dollars, just time. How much is your time worth? Are you trapping cash full time, part time, because you have another job, on a whim, to go shopping, to be a millionaire? Only you know your motives.

It also depends on the outside resources you use to trap cash. Are you at home in your PJ's, or do you have travel expenses that need to be compensated, like transportation, food and lodging? All that's a factor. You may have had to hire someone like an expert on appraisals, inspection, contractors, driving companies, or tow companies. These aren't always the case but must be considered. If you broker a load for a truck driver to transport sweet seedless watermelon from Nogales, Arizona to Sacramento, California, you may have to advance the cost of fuel or just a base advance so the load can be delivered and you can Trap some cash. You may have to grease a few palms for some inside info, or whatever you need to make Trapping your cash just a little easier on you.

## Section 3—Investments

When you look at the cost or "investment" into Trapping Cash, you have to first look at the ability it has to contribute to your bank account, or you and your family's well being. I don't even think about the time I spend Trapping Cash because I love it. I do it all the time. Even in my spare time! I do it to have fun and don't mind doing it on vacation. It doesn't stress me out. I love cash and even the art of Trapping, or the pursuit thereof, is addicting.

Like me, you too, will have some notable moments and once you have a strong network and everybody knows their positions it gets easy. It's like not even doing anything at all and your Traps continue to Trap large profits. It's unbelievable! Sometimes you can get somewhat bored but who's complaining right. Besides time, I may have to invest cash. I never have a problem investing, say $5,000 to make $50,000 or even $500 to make $800. Remember, I'm always thinking tiny.

I'm happy just to Trap a profit, any profit. I really have a thing for $100 bills.

They're lucky to me because it brings me back to my frugal roots, also because of Benjamin Franklin. He's one of my idols. He encouraged all Americans to be industrious, frugal and practice thrift. Thrift is from the same root word as "thrive" – to grow & prosper. He is considered one of the major inventors of the American Dream. Ben Franks as I call them are a constant reminder to me to remember to think tiny.

You should never be losing any sleep over an investment you make into Trapping Cash. You may need to make a few tiny adjustments. "No Worries" is the motto. Everything else in life drains you of cash and time you will never get back, like houses or cars. When Trapping Cash, avoid all extremes, everything is done in moderation.

"We're still inching ahead but we're inching." Warren Buffett (Billionaire Investor)

## Section 4—No Equipment, No Excuse

You can never use equipment as an excuse for not Trapping Cash. You can go from zero dollars to thousands with a pen and a pad of paper. Like I said before, we didn't always have the mobile computer capabilities we have today. I would take a pen and a pad of paper on a clipboard. The clipboard was just for added effect so I really felt important. With that clipboard I would go and search for all the cars for sale within a ten to twenty block radius, write all the full details about them down and that was my cardealership. It wasn't until later when I sold a few that I was able to have pictures and door-to-door flyers and business cards. Yes, I sometimes wore a cheap suit when I met with my customers. I did so well; I took over a larger radius and even quit my job at Popeye's chicken, where I worked as a cook. Thus, was born my first neighborhood consignment car lot.

Many people take the need for equipment way too far, always wanting the best computer or running around finding the newest operating software. A pad of paper just isn't good enough; they need a fancy recorder of some kind. That's like being so caught up in buying a Greyhound ticket that you miss the bus. "Man, when I finally get all this fancy equipment and set it all up, I'm going get absolutely nothing done." It's kind of like slaving in a hot kitchen all day preparing a great meal, but by the time you're done, you're not even hungry anymore.

Too many people get so carried away or engrossed in the wrong part of the process. If they would have put all that energy and excitement into Trapping Cash, they would have never looked back. If I would have gone any further than a pen and my clipboard, not to mention my cheap suit, I would have never got my first consignment car lot, then later, added a "Quick Stop Lube and Tune, plus a car wash. We even ended up buying the property behind us for pennies on the dollar and built a self-storage facility. The car dealership still exists today and is full blown with brand new cars for sale coming straight from the manufacturing line in Detroit to the consumer. I will be the first to tell you technology is breathtaking and so incredible. You have to stand in awe by the things you can do today and it's only getting better. Just don't attempt to speed things up or make them too easy that you hinder your true cash trapping capabilities. "It's not a free ride." Do you get the point?

Technology is a ride to get us there, but it's not going trap cash for you. Good equipment is not necessary but it can be beneficial if you can afford it. The mobile capabilities make it possible for you to trap cash from the backseat of a taxi, or in a hotel, on an airplane, in church, at a concert, during TV commercials and even while meeting with other clients, "can you give me one second, my daughter's calling." The bottom line here is when it comes to trapping cash you don't need all the fancy stuff. I used to go down and use the computer at the public library and trap cash by the truckloads or even use the local senior center. They always have a free business center available at the public library. I used to stalk the business sections and make conversations with other businessmen to find new ways to Trap Cash. I used to think the senior center was just a place full of old geezers where I could take advantage of the computers but boy was I wrong. I walked into a gold mine of information once I took some time to have a conversation with one of the old cats. There's a saying: "If you want to know what's ahead, just ask those coming back." The whole time I was always just in and out on the computer. I was amongst all those old dogs, retired and some very much still active, in business— business owners, lawyers, entrepreneurs, and consultants, some that had made the transaction into being their own boss multiple times. Some even before I was even born! I never knew it, but they had given me the nickname ''Flash'' because I was in and out so fast, they gave me gems of ideas, information on many subjects for free. I told them because I was there more now, "This was my secret spot." They asked me to meet them at their "secret spot." They said they thought it would help me out. It was their golf course! That's where all the businessmen and women were hiding. A place where most deals are made in business behind the scenes, they even gave me golf lessons free! I'm in!!! No equipment necessary!

# Alfred Harvey

## Section 5—You Are The Secret To Your Success

Ninety-five percent of all business and moneymaking success is just showing up! Yes, just showing up. You are an original, trust me. You have something to offer. Yes, you! New and fresh, fascinating ideas. Something that's on your mind, heart and chest, that just you know. No one can read your mind or appear in your dreams and say wow! That's magical! We're going to trap millions of cash and create millions of jobs. You can offer something on a huge scale or even on the tiniest level that can be the difference between making or breaking an idea. You, you, you! Nobody has been everywhere you have been, read what you have read, researched, gathered, assembled, organized what you have, traveled here or there or had your certain experiences. That's what makes you think the way you do. One person can always trap cash alone, but it's a network of trappers that can strengthen, reinforce, shape, and decorate a cash trap to be even more effective.

So make sure you always show up in the chat rooms, auctions, lien sales, swap meets, trade shows, lectures and seminars, not the ones from TV with the guy driving the Rolls Royce, that's surely a scam! But not all of them are, some take place at hotels or conventions centers and are a great way to network and share information, or just to pick up material which may be useful to you.

Television, to me, is a form of LSD or acid that burns into your skull.

Many infomercials take advantage of people not used to showing up at a business convention or a reputable lecture or seminar circuit. Some are free. Some charge a few dollars for entry. But you will see they're well worth it and really will do a lot more for you than the guy with the perfect teeth yelling at you, "quick, grab your credit card and call right now!" You will never know unless you show up. "I think if you're out there hustling, you can find business," stated General Electric CEO, Jeff Immelt.

# CHAPTER 3

Alfred Harvey

## Section 1—The Fanatic

The one who gives your business a reason to exist. You must know the nature of your consumers. Yes, I like to call them fanatics. The person possessed by an excessive or irrational zeal. Not to mention they are the ones holding that cash you wish to trap. It's in their pockets, in their wallets, in their purses, down in their socks or shoes, it's in their hands, it's in their bras, it's in their cars, the glove box, the center console, the ashtray, under their seats, in their trunks, it's at their houses on the counters, in drawers in their closets, under their beds. In safes, even buried in their back yards or in huge bank vaults.

This is the sole individual you will have to become, an expert at satisfying. It doesn't matter if you're trying to trap cash from industrial or commercial consumers. Everyone buying and selling worldwide are trapping cash from one another. It's the art of supplying the ultimate consumer; which is everyone. It's so easy the cavemen were doing it. It's been proven that even our ancestors were trapping cash.

So, you have to get in where you fit in and know how to satisfy as many fanatics as you can, because they are your pride and joy. You want to always keep them happy and give them their way. Spoil them rotten! They will always be right and never wrong. You want to keep them as loyal as you possibly can. You want to be able to attract them by the masses. It doesn't matter if on an occasion or two, one of these little fanatics comes in and takes the cash out of your trap without asking. Just keep a smile and comply. That's what we have insurance for.

Always carry on with business as usual, rain, sleet, or snow. They are your babies.

Love them! You want to know what they like, dislike, what they want, need and their true aspirations. You want to help them in any shape, form, or fashion. It's their world you're just a squirrel trying to trap a nut. Most fanatics have to work for a living because their wants and needs are never completely satisfied and the cash used to satisfy them is limited by nature.

Fanatics all share the common basic needs of food, shelter, and clothing. Those needs may be satisfied in a variety of ways. The more cash a fanatic has, the more they need. It is true; a fanatic can never work hard enough to satisfy every want they have. You have to know what it is they truly desire. Every area has a standard of living that reflects those fanatics, reasonable aspirations in striving for a degree of actual satisfaction at what level they wish to live. Some fanatics are willing to do whatever it takes to get to the level of living they desire.

You have to know how they eat and how you might be able to trap cash by satisfying their irrational appetites. There are laws that generalize their eating habits. As their cash increases, they spend less on food. They persistently spend on shelter and clothes, only increasing what they spend on all other items.

Being able to predict the most likely choice a fanatic will make has trapped billions. Some with more ease than others because they themselves are fanatics as well. The more a fanatic chooses to bust ass at an inconvenience in order to satisfy more wants, this keeps it very possible for us to continue trapping large profits.

Sadly, some fanatics go mad and spiral down to a long blissful debt. Don't be alarmed if your psychic capabilities don't seem to be working. We all have that problem.

Most of us trapping cash just give it a knowledgeable guess and gamble on the result. Many fanatics are blinded by the vast options that are available. So it leaves them indecisive, and an aggressive salesperson, or even an advertising campaign, can bait or influence using creative problem solving techniques. Know yourself and it betters your chances of predicting someone else's actions.

Alfred Harvey

## Section 2—Keep it Real!

I am constantly asked, "How do you trap so much cash?" My easy answer; "I love people and I travel a lot. That's all I need!"

Stay true. Have respect and love for your customers. Show virtue and integrity. Like I said before, they are the reason you are able to trap profits. They are contributing to the level of living for you and your family. So anybody that assists me in bringing home the groceries to feed my family I am forever in debt to.

Your energy is very important in retaining the loyalty of your consumers. You never want your reputation tarnished as a shady businessperson. Word of mouth is the best advertiser. It spreads like wild fire and negative words travel faster, so you must be sincere and not deceitful. Always speak justly, fair and steer clear of gossip because just the word hisses like a snake. Allow everyone to see you practicing to use only one face even though most of us have two.

Be neutral to trifling conversations. Customers don't always believe in second chances. So be sure to go out of your way to assist them the first time around to the fullest of your capabilities. Bend over backward and find a loophole. I'm willing to jump through hoops and even juggle if I have to just to trap cash. "It's all good." Consumers will always remember your flexibility and spread the word to others.

Here's a joke. What do you do when you accidentally call a person who is fake? Hang up is the answer. You probably didn't think this joke was funny. . . Exactly. Being fake isn't either.

## Section 3—What's Your Motivation?

Large stacks of cash! Bundles of it! Bank rolls! The rewards, the wages, the salary, the gargantuan profits, the purses, the huge pots, bread, wads, gwap, avocado, ducats, cheese, deniro, rubies, notes, tender, money, incentives, cream, mint, currency, dollars, chips, greens. Big faces, Ben Franklin's, Benjamin's, confetti, tips, allowance, commissions, and benefits. Don't get it twisted! We all know what motivates us. You can lie to yourself if you want to, the opposite would be broke, and nobody in their right mind would want that. Some people may say, "But at what price are you willing to pay?" Who said anything about paying anything?

It's my money. I'm going hide some and spend it here or there, wherever I see fit.

Ladies and gentlemen, Trap as much cash as you can! Take it from my father, a private decent fellow. A Vietnam Airborne Ranger veteran wounded in combat, worked for the Veteran's Administration Hospital, (V.A.) and winner of the hands and hearts award.

He was on his job for over thirty years until he fell out at work and had a seizure and was forced into retirement. A short time after that, he looked at me with his serious face I've known my whole life and said, "It's all about the money" Wow!!!

OK pops, just relax. I'll check the traps from here on out. He's still going strong and doing well. It's always a joy to hang out with him when I'm not trapping cash.

## Section 4—You Might Want To Get Up!

You're going have to get up at some point to trap that cash. I made it a point to stand more while I wrote this book. It's an abnormal condition, which I believe does impair us. I mean, I'm no health nut but I probably should be. Studies are showing constant sitting for long periods of time has been connected to severe health issues such as heart attacks, stroke, cancers and diabetes. Government studies are saying more than half of us are sitting more than seven hours out of the day at the office, on the couch or in the car. That's way too much sitting and we're not even adding the time we're laying down. Wow. Get up!

Alfred Harvey

# Section 5—Power Points

1.   What are you into? What loosens your body and pumps you full of energy and gets your blood flowing? You want to know this because certain things that drive you wild may drive others the same way. Think! Think! Think!

2.   Your feelings, your gut instinct, is all you! Not everyone feels what you're feeling. You have to understand what your feelings are trying to tell you and go with them.

3.   What do you seem to be better than most at? It's very important to know what your super powers are because it will only push you forward.

4.   What do you feel you're the worst at or that everybody else always beats you at? Doesn't matter because you can always somehow turn it to your advantage.

5.   You are an expert at something. What is it? Everybody is into something and sometimes many things.

6.   Are you outspoken around people? Love to give your opinion? Or are you so shy you can never take your sunglasses off? Do you like eye contact? Again, it doesn't matter. You will still succeed.

7. What intrigues you? This can push you to a passion project. That may come from your soul and bring you happiness and lots of cash.

Whatever your answers or thoughts were on these questions, there are no right or wrong answers. I just came deep from within myself and wanted to get your mind ticking before we move on.

## Section 6—I Know You're Ready!

Who cares what I know. It's about you and your choice of direction, because no matter what you do, you're going trap cash. I'm getting anxious and am already feeling proud of you. I really am. I have that antsy feeling as I'm writing this that you're going trap cash. You're going trap cash! You're going trap cash! You're going do it! I wish I could watch you and see you transform and everybody notice with their mouths wide open. Your energy is booming and they want to know what has gotten into you.

You got some hustle in you now! Well, if I watch you too much, it would probably creep you out or distract you so just contact me and let me know. You're going trap cash!

A Dollar earned today is always worth more than a dollar earned tomorrow.

Alfred Harvey

## Section 7—Getting Started

You already have in your mind or heart something you would like to make a living at. *I am* going to trap cash with it! Not *I would* have, or *I should* have and *I could* have. Woulda, shoulda, coulda is not gonna work for us here and there's no such thing as I'm waiting for this or that. Not even waiting for a friend. Listen, at this rate, it never happens.

Take this little test answering yes or no.

1. Can I really do business on my own?

2. If I don't have anyone supporting me, can I do it alone?

3. Do I have the energy?

4. Can I back away from all the things I like to pass time with like T.V., talking on the phone, web surfing, etc.?

5. Do I have it in me to just go for it?

On this test, not everyone gets a trophy. All your answers should be "YES," for all of the above and if not, no worries, by the time we're done, they will be.

Alfred Harvey

## Section 8—Now Is The Time

You can't wish and want. At that pace, you will never trap cash. Cash trappers do one thing, trap cash. The big secret is making, saving, and spending money. It's a fact, once you get started, you can't stop ever! You just get better and better, greater and greater, faster and faster. I have a buddy who never had "the drive" after he didn't make it into the NBA because of injury. He was somewhat blah, blah when it came to any big step in life. He would sit down in his basement and play video games and puff cigars. Me being a go-getter who stayed in the belly of the beast, when I wasn't checking, tending and setting my cash traps, we would hang out.

I would tell him he needed to get moving and get up, but instead, he started getting heavier on the booze.

He would dream about where he wanted to be in life. He had envisioned it in his head.

I mean I believed in him, but wasn't sure he believed in himself. Every time I talked to him, he would get super duper excited about one of his ideas. I would be like, "That's what's up. You can do it!" Then I would stop by and he would be passed out drunk in his backyard with the dogs licking his face. I mean, I will be honest with you; a few times, I was back there, out cold with the dogs licking my face, too.

He had this idea for a discount sports apparel store. But, since his wife at the time was the only breadwinner, even though it was a great idea, it was just too unlikely. He stayed in a dream state with no action. So one time when we were back in that back yard and couldn't walk, I said, "You know what, man?"

For whatever reason he didn't answer back.

I said, "I think you need to start thinking just a little tinier, like work out of your house or swap meets on a land lot, shared space even, or mobile. I wasn't able to finish speaking my piece because I was being dragged out like a soldier would another soldier wounded in battle, by my very disgruntled wifey. She really got perturbed when I had no explanation on why I didn't call to say I was okay. Plus, I kept singing the Spider Man jingle all the way home.

It wasn't until about two weeks later while I was down in New Orleans for a tiny entrepreneur's conference that I heard my friend had launched a mobile sports apparel store called "injured Reserve." He was attending games from high schools to the tailgate parties in the pros. "Injured Reserve" got an even bigger buzz when it was known most of the workers were injured athletes or at risk youths. It wasn't hard to spot the mobile store because of its colors. People called it the Spider Man Mobile. So, it goes without saying that my friend must have heard me in that backyard.

His success is really showing with all the big boy toys, cars and better house. It even saved his marriage. He told me he just decided to stop playing and trap some cash. We both laughed. He still praises me to this day for the inspiration, but it was all him. He just needed to know he could take the smaller steps. "You can't just talk about it. You have to be about it."

Alfred Harvey

## Section 9—Make The Time

You're going have to make the time to trap cash. I know how hard it is when it seems you have a million things to do, but no matter what you have to get done on your to do list, you can't help thinking about what you need to get done, want to get done, or should get done. Your list will only get bigger. In trapping cash, there's only a small spark needed. I'm telling you once you get that first grand made from your tiny system or network, you will be fired up and you will make the time like you do for everything else you really want to do. Don't you find the time to do the things you really want to do? If you want to trap huge profits bad enough, you will. Period! You're going to have to want it really bad.

You will never find the time. It doesn't matter if you're a part time student, retired, without a job, a homebody or a video gamer, you can only make the time. Trapping cash has to be your number one priority. You have to make it your way of life.

You will find that you will still have all the time to do what you have to do. You will be able to trap cash at the same time you do everything else with just a little multitasking. You will have that super energy if you trap during your daily grind.

"You just have to want it bad enough."

# Alfred Harvey

## Section 10—I Make Time To Trap

I trap everywhere and when I say everywhere, that's just what I mean. Everywhere! When I'm traveling, when I'm speaking, when I'm eating, in church, out with friends, even while I'm in bed. I always make time within my schedule to trap cash. I make sure it fits into my other responsibilities, like chasing my oldest daughter through the mall while she shops for lots of things she doesn't need.

Today I woke up at 5:00 AM in a Holiday Inn in Phoenix, Arizona. At 10:00 a.m. I'm scheduled to enlighten single parents at a conference and workshop on how to use any available space they have to trap profits on a budget. So right now, I'm bouncing off the walls from coffee, listening to music, moon walking back and forth from trapping cash on my I-pad while eating, and writing this book for your enjoyment. Good morning sleepy heads! Getting a bit too wild, I just banged my toe . . . shit! I just got an instant message saying I made $1800 on a goose down pillow deal. That was just a bulk of samples I have to test the waters.

I don't know whether to be happy or in pain (shaking my head). It seems my inside scoop was right about those pillows, so I'll go in heavier next time. If I can't get an electronic signature, I will send one of those notaries I use out to ensure a safe and honest transaction. That was just on a whim and very unexpected. I really do trap any and everywhere; and since that's the way I do it, I always have my thinking cap on for new opportunities, and stay brainstorming with other trappers. Who knows, a trapper in Texas might be having some success at something and wishes to share it. Happens all the time.

Sometimes you can know how things are going with something before you spring your quick trap for cash. Take this book, for example, I knew I wanted to do it, believed I could do it, felt I should do it, but didn't know when I'd do it. It's a fact, writers of books, most of the time; don't make a lot of money on their work. Even some of the well-known authors don't profit the way some people may think. So, it was on the back burner. I was constantly, constantly, constantly asked by my family and friends, some of those I would even be willing to partner up and trap cash with, like complete strangers, retirees, single parents, students, ex-felons, couples, those divorced, immigrants, etc. They have asked me so many questions like, "How do you do it? What do you do? You seem to always have free time! What kind of business do you have? Can you show me? Can you help me? Are they hiring?" Again, you think of it, I've been asked it. And even after I spoke at different functions and people liked my message and wanted to network with me on even on the tiniest level. They would ask, "Hey can I get a contact on you? I really liked your message and where is your book?" I would stand there with my shoulders raised and felt like saying, 1 hey, sorry, I'm just here to paint the hallway.1 My heart goes out to everyone, even to my friend I never called back.

The economy is always in a recession of some kind. Plus, everyone I meet, I truly believe, has the potential to be recession proof and succeed in trapping cash. I like to provide them with a starting point of reference to assist in pushing them to their full potential to trap.

Alfred Harvey

## Section 11—How to Set Up A Mobile Office

Wherever you go your office should always follow. That's what makes trapping or checking your traps for cash possible. We are in the age of mobility with everything including your office. So you can work on planes, trains and in automobiles. The mobile capabilities are only going to get better. Now you can get about the same work done with a few office supplies and one or two gadgets and gizmos. Right now, I'm going over work notes and some speaking preparations and checking any, and all updates and refreshing lists.

I even have a partner in my car on Bluetooth talking about what the Lakers are going do to Boston.

My wife and Ocean just popped on video conferencing and are saying "Hi!" to daddy!

I told her what happened to my toe. She laughed and said, "That's what I get for trying to dance." I hung up on all of them because they all started laughing at me even baby Ocean. So now, you don't have to be cooped up in an office just to advance your business interest. Stay ready so you don't have to get ready. You just need a briefcase or bag that you can carry what you (not another business person) need to handle your business and check your traps.

You can make your own or they have ready to go office supplies for the traveling businessperson. I do a little condensing, but I always have:

1. My clipboard (it's something about having one that makes me feel important)

2. Pads of paper

3. Paper clips

4. Highlighter, pens and pencils

5. Calculator

6. Mini stapler and stapler remover

7. Manila file folders containing several of my business projects and traps that I'm constantly studying.

Those are my lucky seven and I can run a business with just those. Recently added to my portable office to keep up with the times, I have added a Smart Phone and a computer pad with data services. My sixteen-year-old daughter is constantly giving me lessons to use it with more efficiency. So, the small time city boy turned entrepreneur, who was just interested in making a few odd dollars; goes global with the help of a teenage girl. The new technology makes it a lot easier to organize, network, record thoughts, get information while traveling, listen to music and socialize. I also use versatile and flexible apps for outsourcing goods or services. You will learn something every day. I only tip my hat to Silicon Valley. You always have to remember your smart gadgets work for you. You pay the bill! So, just make sure they're doing just that.

Have them personalized to your needs and it will make things easier.

Alfred Harvey

## Section 12—Don't Worry Yourself About Failure!

You have to love failure because it teaches you and it will only make you stronger.

It will also, from the lessons you've learned, prevent you from cracking under pressure in the future. It forces you to have to get up after being knocked down and it's always a learning experience. Many business people and inventors have failed on numerous occasions. We all know human error is unavoidable.

We are not perfect, but failure has pushed some of the greats into stardom at their final success. You will keep learning something new from each failure you experience.

You will have the ability to jump right back in the race and try again, this time stronger. Failure is your teacher, teaching you determination to Trap as much cash as you want. Entrepreneurs, athletes, and musicians have all had to accept failure and learn from it, while strategically coming back stronger, tougher, and smarter.

Failure builds leaders. It's called the 'school of hard knocks'.

Nothing ever comes easy and there is no easy way out. They don't let emotions win, when they fail. They have no shame because they gave it their all. Most of them can't wait for another chance to give their all again. It's always worth the failures to achieve your goal. To Trap cash, you have to know how to turn a bad into a good. Having anxiety, worrying, or uneasy feelings about failure are useless and will only stress you out. We already know the effects stress and strain has on all of us. It is said to be the number one killer in humans and that's not good.

Studies have shown that around 45 percent of what tends to worry us won't even happen. Thirty percent we can't help because it already happened. Ten percent are other people's business. Nine percent are health related, real or imagined. So only six percent of the things we worry and stress over are likely to even happen. No fear!!!

## Section 13—Screw Distractions Keep Going!!

Anything can be a distraction. You have to, at all cost, avoid them. Nothing can be more important than Trapping profits that are used to enrich your family's well being. You have to concentrate and not let people, places, or things, stop you from accomplishing your goals.

If you let them, they surely will! Many people, for some odd reason, don't want to see you achieve your goals. They don't want to see you shining like a star or the happiness from the profits you are able to Trap. A lot of the times it's people that should want you to be happy, like family or friends. Success has its way of bringing envious haters who may have not made the decision to move forward with their lives in a prosperous way.

They will rely on you more once they know that you're the boss and make your own hours. Part of being a Trap Star is being extremely focused on the process at hand. Anything can be a distraction: family, friends, neighbors, even an ex-spouse, the TV or phone, don't let them! You're going to have to focus, focus, focus and don't stop Trapping cash ever!! "Don't stop, won't stop,, can't stop"!

Alfred Harvey

## Section 14—Stay On Your Grind

Like most of us reading this, our love for Trapping cash didn't start today. It started when we were kids in school. I was a true believer in educational freedom and studied independently. All I cared about was the different genius ways I could Trap cash and get rich quick. Trapping cash gave me a sense of power. I could always count on cash and wanted lots of it whenever I needed it. Most of us feel the same way when it comes to cash. There's an entrepreneur that lives in everyone's heart, and there's no telling when it will explode. Boom!!!

It could happen anytime when you least expect it to. It can happen at anytime, at any age, or in any place. It's just that inner happiness and sense of freedom we all yearn for. You just have to do it and you will know when the time is right. Like you, I have worked for someone else before. Once you have experienced entrepreneurship, it makes it a lot harder to be an employee. I would rather run a hotdog stand on the corner than be clocking in everyday and dealing with all the office politics of being employed by someone else. Plus, most of the time we spend working long hours could have been better spent working for ourselves with less stress, more money earned in less time, and more time spent with our families.

A dollar made on your own where you keep a larger portion of it feels so much better than a dollar made for someone else. They just toss 5 cents at you. In some cases not even that when it comes to overall profit. I came from a very tough love environment. When I made my first buck, I was amazed. I knew my father worked but I had made this doing my own work I was a professional now and couldn't nobody tell me different, still can't!

It was like an animal having tasted blood for the first time. I was hungry for more!

I read, I studied, as I got older, I attended entrepreneur boot camps, workshops, conventions, and conferences (not the ones where it seems they won't stop fast talking you to buy what they feel will make your dreams come true). But I loved learning how the big dogs were paid and also how the tiny guy continues to thrive. I learned that you have to grind until you can't grind any more. Pursue cash the way you would anything else you really want. You have to stay at it and you will be surprised how it will all come together like you wouldn't imagine. Grind! Grind! Grind!!!

"The greatest feeling you will have is when you realize you really are your own boss."

# CHAPTER 4

Alfred Harvey

## Section 1—Research, Dissect and Select

Yeah, get your knife out because you're about to have to cut something and possibly break it down to its tiniest form. The second we decide to trap cash we start over thinking, worrying and stressing ourselves out about what kind of business and how we will research, dissect and select the perfect business for ourselves. Relax, relax . . . Most of us are by nature very nosy. Haven't you ever heard the saying, "In business, curiosity made the cat filthy rich!" It sure did. I've seen it many times even the old bird. Our eagerness to know can be a great advantage to us.

Before we get cracking, remember something I said earlier, about only 6 percent of what we worry about is even likely to happen. So just chill, you're going have some fun! Before, I used to go out into my wonderland and marvel at all the different business opportunities that I would be able to spot that no one else could, because I am an original. Everybody, and I do mean everybody, sees something new or fresh or even how to improve something already existing.

I would grab a couple of my great tasting cigars and make sure I had my portable office because I knew I was going need my fancy clipboard. Before I left, I would have a couple glasses of wine just to loosen me up. I do breathing exercises to get the oxygen to my brain, inhale through my nose, and exhale through my mouth. A few basic stretches to get the kinks out and some blood circulation. Always remember to drink responsibly! You will be fine with two glasses of wine or a shot of, say whiskey, just to loosen up and relax you a bit. I made the mistake one time by having one too many vodka martinis with the extra olives and wow! I was everywhere, after happy hour is never the best time! Let me tell you, I ran amuck through the whole city, way too much energy.

I remember looking and analyzing everything under the sun. I was laughing, talking, and even hugging some of the other business owners. I was making so many connections and gaining some super duper ideas. I had so many discussions with different people about what was missing and what would be great ideas.

I had other merchants and vendors breaking things down to me on how things were done, how they got into their business, and the different ways they wanted to expand. I talked to people about recently closed businesses and why they felt they went out of business. I talked to, hugged and welcomed foreign business people who came here as immigrants and now offered a good or service to trap decent profits. I somehow met a new friend and after a few drinks, he shared my passion to trap cash and joined my quest. Now we were everywhere. We hit every swap meet in town, we caught the bus here and there, even visited city hall thinking there was a chance we could meet the mayor. Who would know the city better than him? He is the mayor of the city, right?

When that didn't work out, after a long day of hustle and bustle, I ended up down by the railroad tracks, a well-known spot for all the winos and stumble bums. I sat there listening to how each one of them had or still did own their own business or was a CEO for a great company. I even witnessed a few fights and arguments over whose corporation was the largest. That was until out of nowhere walked up my wife with a look on her face that could have chopped my head off. I never knew or could find out how she could always find me, but she had her ways . . . (coming to take Spiderman home). It wasn't until later I realized I had lost my fancy clipboard with all the great ideas and notes I had taken down that day. Remember, this is the way I did it, and do it. Some of the big boys in business (whoever they are) will tell you their way, but you will always have to adapt to "your own way." This is "a way" not "the way" to Trap Cash. The world is yours!

# Alfred Harvey

## Section 2—Selecting Traps

When you are collecting different ideas for businesses you would like to use as your trap to stack large profits, there's no rush. You're not racing against the clock.

Don't try to put a deadline on yourself because you will only get discouraged. If and when you can't meet the frame of time you've set. When you start and finish it will all come together. Just take to it like a fish does to water. It will just happen, trust that! Be mindful while you swim.

Some things you think will take a day end up taking five, or some things you thought would take a week only take two days because you really got rolling. Time frames will make you race and you have to understand different things, when you're trapping cash will take different times. But eventually you will know what takes a half a day or what takes forty-five days.

Working with my kids when they weren't in school, I loved it! I ended up getting a location and then after a while, sold it, when someone made me an offer I couldn't refuse. He trapped huge profits! He included his great ideas and expanded.

I also have other businesses that still aren't done, like a buy back service for people who already know they are going take a loss, to a tow yard, pawn shop, storage facility, repair shop, etcetera, are able to sell their ownership to the service for cash and even have a longer grace period to buy their items back. It's been around six months since I got the thought and started to research. It just ended up on my back burner. I have a bunch of them. I am constantly trapping cash so I'm always adding new business ideas to my files. I add to them, take from them, sell them, partner up on them, give them names, and get any kind of information on them I can.

I talk to everybody I can. All kinds of experts and I know once I'm done they're going trap huge profits. Always start collecting and writing down your business ideas. As soon as you think of them, grab a pen and write them down or you will lose them or forget them. Don't wait! I'm serious it's a huge waste.

## Section 3—Gathering Your Ideas

What should you put in your box? Everything that pertains to you trapping cash:

1. Thoughts

Yes, you have all kinds of thoughts that come to you at the craziest, funniest times that relate to you trapping cash. Or even other people's thoughts. I pick everybody's brain! I don't care if the baby is trying to help and just gurgles something, always write them all down on anything you can right then. My daughter Ocean's first word was "trap."

2. Clip It

Anything that has something to do with trapping cash that may fascinate or attract your curiosity that has to do with your business or a new one. Articles, papers, magazines, pamphlets, or booklets, snatch it out!

3. Remarks

So many people will make comments that you can relate to your cash trap, or maybe in some kind of way to other ones in your boxes. You have to listen and take down comments so you can remember what they trigger. Your friends, other business owners, customers, and family. Like I said, the baby may gurgle something that sounds like shoe and after a little research you may see there's a market. So, you're selling shoes next week. Even a criticizing joke someone may throw, get it down because you will have the last laugh. It could turn out to be a humorous business name. Who knows?

4.  Studies or Stats

There is always data from surveys or research. Statistics that pertain to your business idea, like how major, how tiny, how great, the worst, the leaders, the losers, how many times, etc. You see!

5.  Research

Research is power! If you at any time feel you're ready, you may be. I've seen people only get about five pieces of paper in their box and they already know, and just go for it. But it doesn't always happen that way. As in my case, my boxes at times are filled. You have got to have a non-stop imagination. Open your mind!

## Section 4—Networking

You have to talk to everyone! There are some very interesting people out there with thoughts, comments, and opinions. They can help you and at times are very valuable with information or experience. You will find their advice can be very important to your cash traps. Trading ideas and even constructive criticism is very healthy to your growth. You can't hide under your bed any longer. Networking is most important. You have to go public and share ideas. I can't stress that enough.

I go manic every time I mention networking because I have trapped so, so, so much cash by doing it. I have been amazed at the people I've met at conventions, conferences, workshops, seminars, and lectures (I'm not talking about the ones where you can't leave without buying a time share, or they bait you in with something free like a toaster, or they say you won a trip that you can only take on a Wednesday). Sometimes you have to say "no," a hundred times and are even haggled all the way out to your car.

I just ignore them and ask my wife, "Baby, where do you want to go eat?" Sometimes, if I'm not sure, if they will have a special interest, I won't even take my wife because sometimes she will get excited about the cruise offer and I got to kick her leg under the table. Sometimes I'll prep her that we're just here to network, period.

If I want to buy something, I will buy it. I don't need someone to try to convince me that I really need something. Someone will even push you into an awkward moment.

Wow! (Shaking my head).

Like I said, there is a whole market of frauds, so I just want you to be on your guard and proceed with caution. Never rush or be rushed into anything like tomorrow's not going come. There are now some circuits or entrepreneur events that will be extremely helpful. Every city has business workshops and lunches that are advertised in the paper weekly. Some places may be free or charge a cover, but very well worth it because they are usually the local business owners or those contemplating going into business. They are very informative and you can find out where and when the large conventions or conferences are, those are truly my favorite. If it's a lecture, conference at a hotel, or even a workshop that is there for networking, (bring some business cards). Some are huge at the convention centers with booths and exhibits. It's like a fair for business and networking. I go to every one I can. Even if it's just to get people's cards and literature.

There are so many different things to see and you can mingle with people at every level of business. There are not just business owners, there are other professional people: doctors, lawyers, teachers, farmers, or stylists. Everybody is there! All I hear is "What line of business are you in?" Someone may say, "I play the drums, I'm in a band, or a grocer. I own a store or Law enforcement I'm a police officer." The list goes on. Where else will you meet a guy having some success in New York at something, now looking to expand in your state or city? Or an inventor who has his great product patented and is looking to sell licensing options for you and me to trap cash.

There's so many people giving samples and showing experiments and networking about this or that. Some will even give great ideas that you can start trapping cash instantly in your area. I've even met some of my greatest partners at conferences or conventions. There's so many booths and neat, cool, things you will see. I've made some amazing connections there that have allowed me to trap major cash. There's so much on-line as well, but there's nothing like in person. Would you go to your county fair online? Exactly! I've had people I met give me inside tips and set me up in business at no cost. That would not have been possible if I was at home hiding under my bed.

The internet is the greatest tool, but there is nothing like in person. Networking is a beautiful thing. If you just so happen to be in California, Las Vegas, New York, Arizona, anywhere just visiting family, friends, or work related, make some time and attend a business convention. It will be worth it. Trust that! When you're networking share ideas and they will contribute to yours as well. There's enough cash for everyone to trap. Force someone to inspire you.

# Alfred Harvey

## Section 5—Many Hands

I have my hands in many different business endeavors. I am constantly checking my traps for profits. You have to strive and thrive. If you're uneasy in the beginning, then just try your hand at one...then, sooner or later, two. A true trapper will always have more than one trap to capture greater profits, but we all started with one or two. At this moment right now, I have ten, and for me the number can change at any time. I've had more than that at times. The more traps, no matter what size, will trap more profits.

You will remember every business endeavor, their different personalities and profit capabilities. At the same time many different products and services you plan to offer. You got this!

Alfred Harvey

## Section 6—You Can Have It All

We don't play! In my father's words, "It's all about the money!" You don't stop life to trap cash; you trap cash while you live life. Don't think, trap! It will come natural after you get it down. The whole lifestyle of trapping cash at all cost.

Period, period, period! Capture, Capture, Capture! Don't let any idea, thought, or comment get away. Clip it, or someone's help, whatever pertains to your cash, get away. Trap it all! You will not always remember, so keep notes. Doesn't matter if you're in church, just step out, trap and God will understand.

Take note on everything you can, napkins, toilet tissue, your hand, your wife, or husband's hand, the wall if you have to. Just don't lose any of it. Get all of it!

Don't worry about studying them right then, just trap them.

Some may seem stupid, wild, crazy, or funny ideas. You will say, "Wow, what was I thinking?" Don't trip. I sure wish I could sit with you and go through all the ideas and brainstorming you come up with because I know, "There's gold in them darn hills."

Alfred Harvey

## Section 7—Right Now

Can you feel the intensity? It's the best time to shine. When we're not talking about what we did in the past or what we're going do in the future, what we are doing right now is what matters. We are in the heart of war with ourselves. Failure, discouragement, depression, and pursuing our happiness. Now is the time to trap cash with all of your six senses. Touch, sight, hearing, scent, taste and your new one, your Trapping Cash mentality. You are unstoppable. You will see!

You can compare trapping cash to having a third eye. After reading this book you will be more powerful than the next person, because you will always be looking through the eyes in the back of your head. Right now, the average person is just looking to see where they can get a doughnut. You will be looking for the tiniest way you can start a doughnut empire right now! People will wonder how did you come up with this stuff. The possibilities are endless.

Alfred Harvey

## Section 8—Sneak In

You have to be everywhere, even uninvited. I would sneak into seminars, lectures, hotel meetings, and company conventions. Any place where they were even talking about a little business or down sizing, even expanding. All different types of meetings that were held at hotels, convention centers, halls, libraries, or city of commerce.

It didn't matter, I was in. I hopped fences, drove right in saying "My name tag got wet" and I need another one. But I always carried a stack of "Hello my name is" tags, I'd get in auction sales, some employee conventions. I wouldn't care if it were for Chicken Hut, I wanted to hear.

It would probably be easier for you to get in. It's harder for me because I have tattoos and piercings. Just makes it harder for me to blend in. But still, I never really had any problems, the bigger the event the better. Sometimes thesebig companies go all out. The food is great most of the time. I mean, I'll be honest with you; a few times I was caught. But hey, we're all professionals here, no reason not to be civil.

I'd know of another boring conference in the building that was open to the public and say, "Oh wow, this isn't the how to bend spoons with your mind conference", and just excuse myself or say, "I was trying to find my wife, she's in one of these meetings. This one is interesting, so I sat down."

One time I told them, "Geez I was just looking for a doughnut." I must say they were always very nice and professional when they profiled me. At times, it was my fault.

I had no business, when the audience was asked if anyone had comments or opinions to come up on stage and speak. There were many great times. I was invited to future conferences and company parties. I was offered jobs. We all went out to lunch many times. At happy hour, you would be surprised at the ideas those who work 9 to 5 will share with you, because most of the time they're too terrified to leave their job and take a risk. We would all be sitting around, eating, having drinks, laughing and I would be asked what branch, city, or state, what division of the company do I work for? They have seen me at their conference the last few days. I finally told them I didn't work for the company and that I was supposed to be attending another conference but it got really boring so I decided to sneak into theirs. That would always erupt the ultimate laughter. "By any means" I still have many friends I speak to regularly

## Section 9—Good For Nothing

I've showed you different ways to casually gather ideas for trapping cash. If you're going to count on others to assist in a more direct way and they don't trap any cash, you're wasting your time. It doesn't work too well. Like, "Hey Vince, I'm going start selling some pretty nice space rugs. Do you ever go to Colorado?"

Vince: "Yeah."

"Well, I hear bear rugs are really popular down there. If you happen to see places where they sell them, could you grab me a few samples and maybe a few pictures?"

Vince: "Yeah, sure."

Well, just know you're not going to get anything from Vince in fifty years even if he marries a bear. Or even, "Hey, would you look over this business plan I've set up and tell me what you think?" You're not going to get anything here either, just hollow "good jobs" (or you might inspire them to trap cash and they ask you to assist them).

The correct way to get assistance is to contact those you know have some sense. Just hit them up online or write them a short letter getting straight to the point. "I'm going be selling hot links on a stick down at the swap meet and I'd like to know exactly what you do while you're

catering events to pack your meat to keep it fresh and safe on the go."
Contact however many you want in the field. Not everybody wants to
be bothered but the advice you do get will prove to be extremely
helpful.

I don't know about you but that sounds good. I'm going to run out and
see if I can find a spicy hot link on a stick. I'm "my own boss." I call
my own lunch. I'll meet you back in the next chapter.

# CHAPTER 5

Alfred Harvey

## Section 1—Enough is Enough

It's time for you to make a name for yourself and your business locally or globally.

It's time to let everyone you meet understand what you stand for and what you represent.

Once you do that, you will have the respect you deserve. You leave them with only one option; they can take it or leave it. It's time to stop playing! We're talking about new eras, dreams fulfilled, proud moments, legacies & sweet victories with real change! Shaking up your critics, never looking back, with solid starts, bragging rights, super swagger, super power, flexing dominance, celebration after celebration, playing your position, creating jobs, making a difference, forging new friendships, hitting the ground running, magic being made, rallies to win & bursting with happiness. Now's the time when you don't worry about anybody else; you have to worry about your own damn self! Everybody else is just going to "hate you enough to want you to fail, and admire you enough to want you to succeed."

It's time to get busy. How can we create more cash? There are many ways. Smart innovative people come up with new ways every day. I'd like to also be the first to say, people who are stupid dumb buffoons come up with the craziest tiny things and it soars to great heights. I think it's safe to say most of us fall in the middle somewhere. Most of the time, their success comes from lots of hard work to sell their products or services. Businesses vary in design. By finding something people want, we're able to trap cash...lots' of it!

## Section 2—Business Face

It will just take a little reasoning and thinking for you to have a perfect business name you would like to see on your sign (if you plan to even have a sign) or even on your business cards with your creative stock and design.

Your ideas can be as good as any graphic designer's ideas, but it won't hurt to hear them out. They may come up with something you like. I would like to give you a few guidelines:

1. Promotion - Immediately promote the type of business in the name to your customers.

2. Attention - Invent a catchy name or a name that will grab them by the ear and pull them in.

3. Simple - The name should be simple to say and easy to talk about.

4. Short Solutions – Ninety percent of the time I made the sale. Most of the time, I paid pennies for the units or they were donated to me when a family had upgraded. For a long time my cards and flyers were free. Most printers will work with you until your business gets going.

I made a deal that allowed the printer to put his service number on the back of my cards and flyers.

You already know when I went to the customers house I would give them a new list of other great things I had to offer and see if they had anything they wanted me to drag away, donate or sell. They would always ask with a smile, "Do you really live behind us?" If there were something they wanted to buy, but I didn't have, I would be the middleman for another seller. As long as I trapped some cash, I didn't care.

Another one of my M.V.P. (most valuable player) cards I had was for car sales. A spin off the Bob Barker (a new car!!!) "All cars within ten blocks of your house." Buy sale or trade any car, any price range call Alfred for a new listing at (my number). That one blew up like an atomic bomb. Boom!!! At that time, I hadn't even owned my own car. But with my success in trapping cash, I sure did get one. I brought a nice Cadillac from a local preacher, my pride, and joy. I was the first one out of all my brothers to get a car. I gave my oldest brother his first Toyota. You couldn't tell me anything, and yes, I kept for sale (bait) signs in all my car windows.

Once a customer called, I would say the one thing they are asking for was sold, but I had many other great cars I'd like to show them. Of course, if they made me an offer for my car that I couldn't refuse, I would get out of it, sign it over to them and walk home. I collected for sale signs. I tried to keep one in the window of everyone's car I knew with my number on it. My parents hated when I put a sign in their car because everywhere they went they would be harassed by buyers. My father later admitted he threw a few of my signs out on the freeway.

Alfred Harvey

# Section 3—Trump Cards

I would choose up to five other businesses that I didn't even own.

I would get business cards and flyers printed up with my name and phone number providing a certain good or service to consumers, commercial or industrial.

I was always communicating with all the local businesses, and since most of them charged different rates to different consumers, I always promoted the best deals. I would be given 25 to 50 percent markdowns for my referrals. I was able to trap huge profits.

At times I would mark up services 20 to 50 percent once I learned all about the promotional discounts, mark ups and mark downs.

Commercial, industrial and even the individual consumer would all pay different rates at different times. Kind of like checking into a hotel. I may check in for $69 a night and you may check in at $150 a night. Rates vary and are subject to change. Many other things may factor in. Customers may need same day service, a weekend or certain day of the week, even after hour service. To go out on a limb is always going cost extra. Small fees are always charged for going the extra mile. Even if they're disguised in other hidden charges.

I would also like to bring to your attention the money wasted by these

Goliath companies all the way down to small businesses. That alone has to be in the billions of dollars. They don't even know what the word frugal or moderation means. I guess they have the money to waste because the ultimate individual fanatic is always tricked in some way or another to pay a higher rate, price, or payment. Most of the time, it's lack of knowledge or laziness to try to find a better price. It's okay because it's huge profit potential for the one trapping cash, to go out and buy a new sweater made from the fine wool of an Asian goat after sweeping up the cash falling off the trees in front of these businesses.

You would be surprised how those put in charge of purchasing or buying goods and services for the large companies. Just squander money. I mean hey, it's not theirs, right?

They're just there to run the clock out. Some companies don't even have a person in charge of purchasing and buying. It's usually done by any employee, supervisor, or manager; sometimes it's the guy taking the trash out.

Flyers or brochures to all my different goods and services amongst those the company used. I would sometimes be the main service used or just put in the wings as an option. Nevertheless, I would trap super duper profits. A lot of the times a company would use different services of mine and not even know they were all the same trap star.

I would offer laundry services to guests at a hotel and not even own a dry cleaner, but because I gave free laundry services behind the scenes to an employee, they would make sure I was on the board, giving free dry cleaning service to one, was always worth gaining 100 plus customers any time. Unless garments were in need of special cleaning, I wouldn't even out source to an industrial wash; they were just washed and processed at someone's home or local Laundromat. You already know any service showing up on your room service bill is always a mark up.

A company's delivery truck could go out and because of a well-put together flyer and business card. They thought they were getting a full service repair company when it was just me outsourcing the job to my neighborhood mechanic, Johnny. I would even send holiday cards to companies who didn't even use my services. Most of my services stay swamped. Yes even today trust and believe I'm on, or behind, the scenes somewhere trapping cash. "It's the art of influence or at times just plain puffing."

## Section 4—I Fly

Flyers and brochures are just as important as business cards. It helps for your goods and services to be recognized by every business and keep you on their radar. Just try it! Make some flyers even if they're fake and you will be surprised at the calls you get. They will always pick up the phone and call. They may even ask is your service office, really? Right up the street from ours?"

There are so many ideas you will have for different flyers or business cards. You're just as good as anyone at putting together the perfect ones. It's not hard at all. Here are a few pointers you can go by:

1. Colors: You want it to constantly pop out at them and have them thinking, what is that? Oh, it's the office's janitorial service; I've been meaning to call them!

2. Basic: You want it to be understood without any thought.

3. Energy: Smiley faces are always good. Anything that can be uplifting in a positive way.

4. Promotions: Discounts, donations being made locally to kids, animals or to another cause.

Alfred Harvey

## Section 5—Do It Yourself Printing

Just a quick point, because of the changes made in printing capabilities, you can do most of the printing yourself at home or on a friend's printer. Just buy the stock and ink and you're in business. I would do a lot of my printing and everybody else's I could find. I would do all the printing for menus, flyers, business cards, signs, banners, brochures, and many promotional products for all types of businesses. Once I took the time to learn the different printing programs, software and taking a quick crash course from anyone who knew what they were doing. I was able to add another business to my arsenal and trap lots of cash.

# CHAPTER 6

Alfred Harvey

# Section 1—You Have to Enter to Get A Prize and clothing for you and your family.

Free enterprise is the mechanism for systematically producing, financing, storing, transporting, and selling your goods. You're probably like most people and me; we have to feed these babies! I refuse to have those beautiful faces looking up at me, like dad, what are we doing? What are we doing dad? I would be damned without free enterprise and a capitalistic system. We all would! You are able to produce goods privately and trap huge profits. *You* have to seize that advantage. *You* are your own boss! *You* have to overwhelm by force, confiscate and trap huge bundles of cash.

It doesn't matter if for 10 cents you buy a bag of apples from a local farmer and satisfy your customer with that same bag of apples for $1.00 or even a $10.00 apple pie. Great job! You always have to be ready to venture. Free enterprise is the first step; you have to take it! It's just like when you stand your precious little baby up and try to get him or her to take those first steps. It's the same thing.

You will get nowhere being introverted or crawling back and forth to the kitchen while you allow Seinfeld or American Idol to burn a hole in your damn head. You have got to free yourself from whatever it is that is holding you back from enterprising. We would be here forever trying to figure out all the reasons or excuses we use for not engaging in our own business. We will stay broke and won't trap a dime. I will give you the number one reason for you not enterprising. It's you! There are no excuses because you are free to enterprise. Engage!

## Section 2—I Hustle ...

For mutual benefit, services, goods and money. Those who are in business for themselves personally exchange goods and services to trap as much damn cash as they can, (Listen carefully this is very important) or they are directly responsible for the exchange.

Professional trap stars live for the next transaction and in many cases are only as good as their last. They strive hard, understanding they are the bosses! With their first steps, they are the presidents, vice-presidents, treasurers, and secretaries. They run all the departments, production, shipping and receiving. They are even the laborers until they decide to hire trusted employees. But until then, it's your job to solve any and all problems and handle the details, being mindful of what you spend for the purpose of trapping gigantic profits.

You have to decide what duties you want to outsource to other businesses if any.

Like I said earlier, some businesses are trapping huge profits out sourcing all goods and services promoted to other businesses never truly being in the business being promoted, acting only through silent referrals. A trap star will constantly gain new contacts and maintain positive relationships with customers as well as others involved in business.

Alfred Harvey

## Section 3—I'm Busy

You got to get your hustle on, period! Get the wind beneath your feet and go out in a blaze if you got to. Business is not always humane, so after you decided this is it and you throw that brick through your big screen T.V. and realize you are the organizer, there's no turning back! Everybody is hustling! You have just joined the race! Give it all gas and no brakes! Floor it!

It doesn't matter who you are, how you look, what you know or who you know, everybody is trying to get paid! Once you understand how to organize and arrange, you will trap so much cash you'll have to weigh it to know how much you really have. Because trust me, you will always lose count and jam cash counter after cash counter. A true hustler knows how to organize and arrange just the way a conductor would an orchestra or a train. Remember what I said, no brakes!

Okay, who wants to get paid? Let's conduct some business! Remember, you may enter into any business you choose. You don't have to be a doctor to own a hospital or even organize a neighborhood clinic. You don't have to be a farmer or own a dairy to organize and operate a local market, which offers fresh milk, fruits and vegetables. You don't have to be a butcher to sell choice meats.

Later, I will show you the value these establishments are to the one organizing and operating a neighborhood consignment market. You will trap large profits when you understand the hustle behind conducting and minding your business. You don't have to be a barber or even know how to cut hair to operate a barbershop. You don't have to be a postmaster to conduct a pack and ship (mail services). You don't have to know how to pick a lock to operate a locksmith service. You don't even have to smoke to operate a full service retail tobacco store. You don't have to be a real estate agent to sell, buy, or trade a house, land or other property. You don't have to have any animals to watch someone's cat, or walk their dogs. Woof! You don't have to be a janitor to organize and conduct a residential or commercial cleaning service. In fact, low cost commercial cleaning services are listed in the top five of low start ups ranging from $500 plus.

They also have a high participation rate among minorities. Non-medical in home care for seniors is number one and is expecting a huge boom! (Listen carefully) There are 79 million baby boomers (born from 1948 to 1964) that will be ready to retire after dominating the senior population. There will be as many old people as there are young people. Twenty percent in each age group compared to 13 percent seniors and Twenty-three percent children today.

So in knowing that, let's get ready to service these old geezers and trap some cash. Everybody is hustling! Pass the word, business cards, and flyers. Word of mouth is the best way to earn new clients. Keep an appointment book, have a dedicated phone line, and always appropriately dress for client meetings. It doesn't matter if you're high pressure washing houses or bidding on storage units.

From my countless hours of study and research, my prediction is we are going to see a boom in the service sector (listen carefully.) "Be ready to catch and ride the wave of *new* and *improved* services being offered to the consumers. Just use your mind and create/invent new services and trap super cash."

Come on now, you'll think of something! "Think tiny." Remember: No matter who you are, most of the smartest people always work for someone else. They will line up around the block with their fancy degrees and certifications, ready to pledge allegiance to your idea, service, or dream, to minimize your risk factor. Unemployment is a growing force. Put them to work! And, my god, there's a lot of them!

Alfred Harvey

# Section 4—Visualize

Vision: a mental image produced by the imagination. It doesn't matter what everybody else is seeing. What matters is what you're seeing! It's very important to visualize and use your imagination and inventiveness in all aspects of your life. There's a lot of power in that light bulb popping on in your head and forming a mental image of what is to come. Before I get busy with a business, I visualize everything completely.

I love to daydream about all the cash I'm going trap. I picture the process already complete. The business, the functions, the art form, everything! I even see myself promoting it like crazy. I go through the whole system in my head.

I'm going have to make it legal, so I see myself going to City Hall or other government agencies for licensing or any other permits I may need. Am I going be alone on this one or will I have a partner? I'm thinking of all the skills I will have to learn, and where I can get some quick crash courses, because time is always of the essence.

I don't want to get discouraged. I'm constantly thinking of all the statistics and business information.

I see myself establishing, organizing, arranging, and conducting the whole time, I'm drooling with a private smile. I control this, I can manage! What kind of cash I'm working with and if I will need any at all? Then the best part—promote, promote, promote. Then I hear my wife, "Alfred, Alfred! I'm trying to talk to you." OMG woman! Leave me alone I'm trying to visualize!

## Section 5—American Business

It's the biggest four factors of production, natural resources, labor, capital and the trapped entrepreneurship or initiative. Yes, the first wobbly steps in establishing, organizing, arranging and conducting *your business*. I don't give a damn if it's a candy house! You have the strongest country in the world with the biggest guns backing you up to assure you have the peace of mind to privately produce your goods and sell them for profits.

You are the owner, you have the cash and you want to trap cash by the busloads, there will be very little interference from big brother, uncle, big daddy, or whatever you want to call them. They will not interfere with you trapping cash; you are free to enterprise.

Alfred Harvey

## Section 6—Hands Tied

You don't have a damn choice! It's either trap or die; your ass is backed in the corner. The future is bleak, you're trying to make a dollar out of 15 cents, and it's hard to pay the rent. In the end when you look for all your friends, they're going to be *blowin' in the wind*. The gloves have to come off; it's survival of the fittest!

All we hear is oh my God they're sending all the jobs overseas. Let them do them, quit chasing behind them! We are entrepreneurs in the United States of America. We are the Kings for years to come. Everything we need to succeed and trap super cash is right here! We breed constant greats. Top schools, solid rule of law, we raise entrepreneur giants, a grand market, no matter democrat or republican, they're all pro-business. We have the ability to reach globally but choose not to leave the block. Wow! You have to use your guts instinct for compensation. China has those who organize and operate but they have no rule of law. Europe has rule of law but has no entrepreneurial culture.

Steve Jobs, the founder of Apple is a prime example of what the hell we got here in the U.S. Pro-business policy, rule of law, and trap stars who operate, arrange, and conduct. We trap major bread, relish, peas, and guacamole baby! It's just what we do!

## Section 7—R.I.P. Middle Class

Middle class is dead! It's just an illusion either you're rich or you're poor, period. Free, or full of death. Oops! I mean debt. Well, same thing. Only the best of the best will earn the big bucks. You have to know how to create jobs, yes including your own. These huge companies will pick your brain and make you believe you're middle class, then you're history. The poor decision will be your own fault. On my God, what am I going do? I'll tell you, you're going do <u>you</u>! You're going to apply philosophy to entrepreneurial strategic thinking about what you would like, want, and need, and start providing that for others who share your views. Trust me, we're out there.

Another illusion is your retirement. A 401k plan is not a retirement plan! You are allowed to take money out after you put it in. Plus, you can borrow from it and you can't take it with you to your new job. That's a joke, not a retirement plan. The truth is, 75 percent of citizens of this country will rely entirely on Social Security, (shaking my head). That worries me. *"We all have to step up."* Obama said.

If you're young with income, then start a Roth IRA. Call Charles Schwab, he'll hook you up!

Alfred Harvey

## Section 8—Low Income Anonymous

Hi, my name is Alfred Harvey and I'm broke! Yes, there is a 12-step program for under earners. I told you I am an ultimate networker. You can also call me an extreme grouper. That's someone who attends many different meetings or groups in the community for no apparent reason other than the fact that I can. I do out of respect, steer clear of the more severe medical related groups because I wear my heart on my sleeve and I already know me. I may come out of one of those meetings without my kidney, or either start buying and selling them as a profession. I made a promise to myself that I would buy and sell everything under the sun that is on the outside of the human body.

But I must say I know a guy who sold one of his kidneys and with the proceeds started a business and is doing really well. I already know what you're thinking, and no,

I promise you it wasn't me. (Shaking my head) After struggling with addiction myself, from everything such as partying with drugs and drinking, to aspiring to be the next Charlie Sheen. So, I'm very aware of the power of groups. I attend all of them that I can, not just business related. Groups for singles, drug addicts, drinkers, widows, divorcees, victims of crime and battered women. I've even dragged my wife out for a few meetings for couples even though I know she would rather be at home watching Basketball Wives, or Love and Hip Hop of Atlanta. "You can just record it, you're going!" She always has a lot of fun, but won't admit it.

I will be honest with you. In the beginning when I first started grouping, it was all about solicitation and let me just say it's a lot better than door-to-door sales.

I would have my business cards and wow, I stayed busy. I would be mowing lawns for couples, I would be cleaning out widow's garages, shampooing carpets, house sitting, fixing things I was able to fix and if I couldn't I would just out source it for a percentage of the profit. I would wash cars, houses, driveways, didn't matter, buy sell or trade cars.

A lot of this business I probably wouldn't have gotten with just door-to-door knocking.

I guess there's just a stronger bond with a person after you've hugged and cried with them. Not to mention the gut wrenching laughter I bring to the table. You would be surprised of the connections you can make in groups. Trust me, everyone there is networking and there is no wrong in it. To this day, when I have the time, I still attend groups and always offer a variety of services and information.

Most of the time, I'm a guest speaker at groups around the country. Still, many of the same groups I have frequented in the past. Now they're just on a larger scale and they're called conventions. It's a passion of mine to be able to inspire a grandmother to sell humorous t-shirts or design coffee mugs, or for a single dad to learn how to buy and sell cars starting with the commissions earned from selling other people's cars. Or how students or ex-addicts can make $300 plus on a Saturday, doing quick exterior only washes within a few block radius, with a high-pressure washer.

There are about thirty houses on one block. You figure the people like me who will pay $20 to $30 a month to come out on a Saturday morning to our cars already polished and gleaming. "Let's go kids; we're going to the beach!" I have recently attended, after being invited by a friend, a group I never even knew existed called under-earners anonymous, for those people who get sad or depressed from the small paychecks they bring home. Some were laid off or suffered from lack of new opportunities. No matter who we are, we want to trap more cash. I mean who doesn't. But since I came from being broke, I fit right in.

We find that a lot of those under earners who attend actually sabotage themselves financially. They compulsively reject ideas that could expand their incomes and increase their personal profitability through business, jobs and other avenues. Under earning, just as well as any addiction, will take a series of meaningful steps. You really have to want to trap more cash. *"When life hands you lemons, make lemonade."*

Alfred Harvey

## Section 9—Owner Sharpens Owner

You are an owner whether you're new, old, educated, or an eighth-grade drop out. If you just realized your position yesterday or last week or been at it for nine years.

You are an owner whether you only make a buck or a million of them. Your office can be at your home, a hotel, and the car, on a plane, on the corner, even on the roof. You are the owner!

We are motivated by self-sufficiency, inventiveness, and growing our masterpieces.

Iron sharpens iron and so do owners. We are addicted to business ownership. Most of us need hustlers anonymous, so we can cry and hug each other on the fact we just can't stop trapping cash. We sharpen each other constantly. (This is very important) Always be humble enough to learn. You can be the teacher, the student, the newbie, or the veteran. If you do not listen, you will learn the hard way.

Even if I know more than the person I am talking to, I always listen very carefully because the person may say one thing that's important that just sharpened my game, and would cause me to say, "Well would you look at the time. It's been fun but I've got to run, we'll do lunch!" I get to my home office and dash through the house, leaving my family puzzled sitting in the family room like, what the hell! Out the back door, I go tripping over the dog and toys, scaring the crap out of the cat, falling and getting back up, getting a grimace from my nosy neighbor next door. "Hi, Ms. Johnson!" Finally getting to my garage door with all my "Keep Out", "No One Allowed", "Trespassers Will Be Prosecuted", Area 51", "Smile You're On Camera", "Never Mind Dog, Beware Of The Owner", "Retina Scan Needed Beyond This Point", stickers all over the door. Yeah, and a few Hello Kitty, number one, and I love daddy stickers. My little girls are something else. I love them to death but they also understand what the "No Kids Allowed" sticker means.

I shake my keys into the two dead bolts and enter my secret micro-factory and dive straight into all my information and research with all the "bang, boom, bang" FX you would hear when <u>Goofy</u> from Disney falls down some stairs in the cartoons. Bang! I finally realize I have the added ingredient I needed for a million dollar idea I have been working on for a while. I don't remember what million-dollar idea it was. It was either the combination of a pacifier or baby bottle with an IPod to download a mother's voice or lullabies to lull a baby during feeding or sleeping.

Or it could have been something to keep my dog busy in the back yard and not digging holes in my tomato garden.

But who would have known a volunteer crossing guard was as

knowledgeable as she was.

I told myself I had to go back to hear more about 3-D design software and photo realistic rendering technology. I must have been thanking her aloud for unknowingly giving me the groundbreaking tweaks I needed for my project, because I heard my wife behind me say, "So who's Alice? Come on kids, we're going to Pizza Jungle!"

Owners sharpen owners on the streets, the parks, the golf courses, the internet, and social networks. You gain valuable insight with a listening ear from peers on blogs, twitter, emails, or web links. It's all guidance, advice, tips, or suggestions. The people I like to call angels will assist you on your path, unless it's a hired consultant. These mentoring angels usually work for free! One of these old baby boomers with all their previous experience and valuable knowledge of the industry you're joining or looking to improve on won't have a problem helping out a young whipper-snapper like yourself succeed.

You could ask them if you could do it all over again, how would you do it? Or, what about this or that? They may even give you ideas they never had the time to pursue.

You must also know not all mentors are old and retired. They're your everyday people, young, middle-aged, and old. All different kinds of professions don't count them out because they may be a police officer, and not a club owner, or a doctor and not one who owns a store, or is a volunteer crossing guard and not a car repair shop owner.

Don't judge a person by their hair cut because every one of those pairs I mentioned could be related by family, geography or culture, etc. You will never know. Don't burn your connections. "When two people see eye to eye, they become the same height."

# Section 10—Fearless and Undaunted

You have got to push forward at all times with no brakes because when you become a serious trap star, you will be observed and have onlookers everywhere. Family and friends will have to get used to the fact that your schedule has changed. Your kids won't be the only ones making a mess. All your research will be everywhere. A lot of new mail coming for you, the phones ringing off the hook for you, you're always on line, magazines, manuals, newspaper, books, and statistics covering every table in the house like you're a mad scientist. It's kind of like a mechanic who works on an engine in the living room. You will come in one day and everybody voted you out into the garage and they won't even have a problem helping you move everything.

When you go places, people will stare and notice you like never before. Even when you're out with family, they will attempt to finish the conversation you guys were having about the pros and cons of "crowd sourcing," come on dad! You will get so tired of everyone asking, "How's the business or invention coming along?" Have you finished that thing you were working on? Everybody will think you're going crazy and losing your mind. Your life partner will be picking the locks to the garage suspecting you of living a double life. People close to you will, out of nowhere, start lecturing you about their perspectives on staying in a marriage and family values. Without losing sight of what's important, "Okay Ms. Johnson, I will keep my dog off your lawn."

It will seem like everyone is judging or evaluating you. Your own mind will even start to have problems separating the brilliant ideas from the duds after talking to those onlookers who hate and are secretly envious, saying things like, "I don't really know about that idea, Alfred." Some people will even lie to you about dud ideas possibly having a chance. You will become upset at others you see trap cash like as if you need to do more.

If you didn't know the meaning of the word "hater," you will now. Whatever you do, don't let others knock you off your path. Never doubt yourself, because you are the core not them. We all go through rough patches. It's a part of being great. Just snap out of it and grind on!

## Section 11—One Man Show

A trap star will not always expect assistance or help with a project from friends, spouses, bankers, coaches, or other business people with loans or grants. Sometime there's help and sometimes there's not. You are on your own, is how you should think, because you never want to not be able to go forward because you can't get this grant, or your spouse is busy.

Your projects are in your *heart* and your *head* and it's going be that way until you hire hands. Yes, there will be times when you feel less confident than you once did about a project. Happens all the time. Keep going! You can just relax when you need to, or sleep on a decision before going that direction. Just make for damn sure that whoever you go to for help is at times, even more passionate than you are. They can build your energy just from brainstorming. You can feel the excitement.

When things slow down for you, it's usually just missing a little inspiration or intelligence and after the huddle you're ready for the play. Sometimes, collaborating with my competition really fires me up. Just by their cockiness, I usually walk away thinking 'Yeah, let's see how you feel when I improve your service and take all your customers!'

Alfred Harvey

# CHAPTER 7

Alfred Harvey

## Section 1—95 Percent is Just Showing Up

I've said this before and I'm going say it a lot more because it is the most important part of succeeding in minding your own business, period! If anyone tells you different, they're a liar, a fat mouth, and the truth is not in them. It's not having a bank roll, it's not having good credit, it's not having other people's money, you will never be in the right place at the right time if you're not showing up. I've hung around other people's businesses just shooting the breeze. I've rode on other trap stars coattails and tried to let them drag me any and everywhere they could. I've had no problem being in the passenger seat or even the back. Shoot, I'd ride in the hatchback if I had to.

Like I said earlier, a bunch of times I would show up uninvited and have to be escorted out. "Hey guys, if I needed roller skates I would of wore some. Get your damn hands off of me." I had no shame. I was always showing up! I would even be at other owner's beck and call. "Sure I can grab your laundry from the cleaners for you." Even if I weren't, I would say, "it's no problem. It just so happens I'm in the area," or "Yes,

Mr. Ingram, I can pick Amina and Amir up from school today and drop them off at soccer practice." Sometimes I'd even have to call my wife and have her pick up our own kids and she would say, "If all your friends jump off the San Francisco bridge, are you going jump too?" I'd get quiet and she would say, "ugh!" then hang up on me. I think she knew I was visualizing myself taking the plunge and holding my nose all the way down.

You have to show up! Your two worst enemies are laziness and procrastination.

They are out to destroy you and usually win a lot more than they lose. But a very audacious trap star will always prevail.

## Section 2—Foolish Lazy Prisoners

We have all been held captive by leisure and we can all learn a great deal just studying the ant, a very tiny and humble creature. Just take it from Proverbs of Solomon, the son of David, King of Israel. Solomon was the wisest and wealthiest man of all time.

Take the richest wisest person today and Solomon makes him or her look like a parking attendant. He says in proverbs 6:6-11, "Go to the ant, you sluggard! Consider her ways and be wise (7), which having no captain, overseer, or ruler (8), Provides her supplies in the summer and gathers her food in the harvest (9). How long will you slumber, "O" sluggard? When will you rise from your sleep (10)? A little sleep, a little slumber, a little folding of the hands to sleep." So shall your poverty come on like a prowler and your need like an armed man."? Nothing comes to a sleeper but a dream." At times, we all need some ants in our pants. I'll see you in the next section. I'm going run out and buy an ant farm.

Alfred Harvey

## Section 3—Natural Observations

Birds of a feather flock together. A lot of us may think because we all have unique fingerprints that we are all in a class of our own. Well, we're not. But we do tend to converse with others in a similar class as ours. Some people seem to be in our league and some people seem to be out of our league. Start with your class, because that's the one you know best. Start naturally observing any and everything. You can improve on things you like or dislike your personal interests. It's harder to do while reading, but you want to be able to realize when you say, "Wow, I wish this service did this" or when you're talking to a person who works for a company and they say, "Sorry, we don't do that." Those are the . . . Booms!

Let's say you're at home lounging in your Obama pajamas and get the thought to go to the store for a pack of smokes, six-pack of beer, and a spicy peppered beef jerky. Or you're too tired after work and you don't feel like getting all the way out of the car for a gallon of milk and had a quick thought, "Wow, I wish they had a drive thru store over here like they did when we lived over in Alta Loma. That would be nice." A trap star, after having that thought would immediately say, "Wait a minute!"

Then while they were pushing a basket through the store in their

Obama pajamas, they would be smiling because they would know that they just thought of something huge, and visualized trapping so much cash. Just observe everything, any class, any place, any time. Somewhere in the zigzag of life, you snare your enthusiasm on an idea. That's when you've found your opportunity.

## Section 4—Limit Your Liability

Just because you're a tiny ant that's trapping huge profits does not mean you can't incorporate like the rest of the goliath corporations. Over half of all small or medium businesses (SMB's) operate under sole proprietorships or partnerships. I highly recommend against this. The extra you will spend on incorporation will be well worth it. It's the best insurance.

You may have had a few great years in business and have stacked up a great deal of personal assets. You want to protect those. Who knows, you may get a sloppy creditor that from the start didn't care if you succeeded or failed and if you by chance default, is not obligated to give you a grace period. I mean it was bad for me to be out back in the pool practicing my cannonballs and having my golden retriever catch tennis balls off the diving board while I'm filming him for America's Funniest Home videos and have my wife run out there and say, "Alfred, a tow truck just took both our cars out of the driveway!" What!

It even got worse when my baby daughter, Ocean, follows her outside with one shoe on and her hair not combed, still unable to speak really well, but was still trying to mock her mother with the "What is going on, dad," look on her face. Even my dog darted in the house looking for the nearest closet to hide in. I just wanted to crawl straight into the pool's filtration system.

Many personal bankruptcies were caused by the failure to incorporate. You can incorporate for a couple of hundred. Don't dwell on the pros and cons like other businesses because it's a no brainer. When your business starts to grow, so will your creditors, so protect yourself. Corporate advantages come in many forms from tax deductions, life, medical, and dental insurance, education, travel expenses, fringes, not to mention worker's comp. The smoothest way to split the company between partners is selling corporate stock. If you plan to use other people's money, you can attract the loan sharks by being very flexible. Just ask any accountant; they will have no problem putting you up on game. Have many of the valuable assets in your own name, not the corporations, just in case of default, those assets will not be on the bankruptcy auction chopping block.

## Section 5—Don't Play Yourself, Pay Yourself

Never do anything for free. Always get paid in full for whatever you do! Always pay yourself! If you spend a dime, expect twenty million in return. Yes, shoot for the stars on this one. Just like what Grandma used to say before she threw the dice, "Dough it and you won't owe it." Couldn't nobody shoot dice better than Grandma.

In any situation, get paid when you make your point. Now there is nothing at all wrong with the non-profit sector, there are many good things going on in this sector. There are a lot of people trapping large amounts of cash in the non-profit sector doing something good for the community or environment all over the world. Business isn't about morals, it's about money. Remember that nobody is doing anything completely for free unless they're feeling guilty, because they have already trapped a huge pot of gold.

It's okay if you decide you want to be paid with a good conscience, I just don't know much about that. Once I experience it, I may put a great book together about it, but as of right now, I just want to be paid in gold or my lucky Ben Franks because those are collector's items if you didn't know. I have a saying, "It's not a free ride." You cripple someone for not making them work or pay for the things they want. I recommend everybody take some time out and go sit in the park with some of those old cats. They will really teach you something. That's one of the places Grandma used to shoot dice. "Dough it and you won't owe it."

## Section 6—S. O. B. (the Spirit of Business)

Do you ever wonder why some people tend to always win a lot more money than they lose? I will tell you why. It's the "Spirit of Business." Every one of the most successful businessmen that come to your mind right now, like the Gates, Trumps, and Buffets, stay filled at all times with the "Spirit of Business." They live it! When it comes to your daily grind you have to get tired of the bullcrap - pockets filled one day and empty the next. Wondering to yourself what it would be like not to have to stress over money issues and just live for a damn change. Hoping for a solution that was easy enough to understand and reasonable enough to attempt?

Have you ever tried to trust in business? Your own business! Yes, I'm talking to you. Your own business. Your business is your friend. Your business will love you. Your business is your future; your business is waiting to give you a brand new life. It's time to make the decision to change up just a little bit. Not enough to frustrate you, but just enough for a small action in your past, to cause a huge change in your future.

You have to challenge yourself just once. Take ownership over some abandoned property. Buy and sell a cheap piece of land, buy a piece of real estate on "short sale", buy just one government property tax    lien, or even get up and go out and bid on one storage unit that's in default in your area. Some self-storage facilities will even let you bid on just one item in a unit, cheap, like a box of who knows what's in it! Go do it once just for the heck of it. Call or get online and find out where in your area the next one is and grab yourself a bag of popcorn and just go watch. Make it a date! I will tell you one thing. I'm not going to stop showing up! You shouldn't either.

Now I'll be honest with you, I don't really care if you do it or not because to tell you the truth, I'm not really into someone I don't know yapping his or her jaws about what I need to do to be happy. Blah, blah, blah! The whole time the idiot's talking, I'm thinking about how great my wife was last night and the fact at that particular moment, I'm craving a cigar!

The "Spirit of Business" will take you over, trust that! It will become fun. I took a friend to a few auctions with me once, and the week following, I got a call from him all excited saying, "What's up Zero?

I said, "Bro, you're on your own. I'm out of the area at a convention." When we hung up, I had a "private smile" because I knew he was filled with the *Spirit* of *Business*. I grew up in a rough, tough love environment and I've learned you can lead a person to the money, but you can't force them to fill their pockets once they get to it.

# Section 7—Meeting of the Minds

Now is the best time to get into business. If you have been doing your homework, taking notes, research, reading the newspaper and watching the news, the present leaders in business and government, also the smartest people in the world are having sessions, summits and meetings about competing in business and creating jobs. Take advantage of the fact that we are back to the basics of, "minding your own business," by Benjamin Franklin, and "Having to step it up," by Barrack Obama.

The inflated dollar has popped! We're over spent! We fell victim to consumerism and mind manipulation. It was fun, but now we have to trap major cash off the correction of self. The leaders are sitting around trying to come up with ideas, strategies, remedies, to create jobs, visions and proposals to completely eliminate the capital gains tax on small and medium businesses (SMB's) and ease restrictions and fees on small business association backed loans. There's opportunity to trap major cash because we're starting over and rebuilding. Troubled Asset Relief Programs (TARP) and recovery acts are being passed. The fed is bailing out all the leaders, banks, housing, car manufacturers, etc. The credit rating is tore up, (S&P); Standard, and Poor says so!

This is your chance to lead, analyze, create, step it up, and mind your own business even on the tiniest level. Trap cash!

This is still the land of milk and honey. I'm seeing all different kinds of people filled with the "Spirit of Business" out trapping cash. The stay at home parent, single or with a partner, students, retirees, the employed, the veteran, the dropout, ex addicts, the recently laid off, those educated, those on welfare, the old, the young, or the disabled. We are not playing. We are out here trying to get it! It's up to you whenever you want to join the club. I'm just saying now would be a great time.

## Section 8—Mind Your Business

Do you know what the motto was on the U.S. currency before the words, "In God We Trust?" No, this is not one of those age-old conspiracy theories. The owl, the eye or new world order that were just put in place to keep us going insane and busy trying to figure out something that means nothing and constantly pulling out our money they created to prove a point. They're just laughing and getting richer and richer.

In 1776, Benjamin Franklin coined the phrase, *"mind your business,"* which appeared on the first U.S. mint to go into circulation. Mind you, at a time when we were in the process of building the greatest business idea known to man, "The United States of America." So it leaves you to ponder why one of the greatest business minds ever would choose that motto to be placed on the U.S. currency that he knew and believed would become the world's strongest and only later to be changed to a motto that the majority of U.S. citizens lean on for support.

But remember, don't ponder too long because they're still getting richer and richer.

Mr. Franklin used *"mind your business"* as the first motto on our so beloved U.S. currency that was to be used as legal tender for any and all debts, public and private in all business transactions. The statement which has multiple meanings, which seemed very popular in those times is a powerful foundation and building block for anyone attempting to go into business for themselves. Let's break it down: *The Mind* where all ideas originate. *Your,* meaning self, and *Business,* meaning profits. Use your mind to create original ideas to trap huge profits. Profit from your own. There's more *security* working for self. Think and grow rich, crate your own job etc. Then on the flip side of the coin, "it doesn't cost you a dime to stay out of mine." So, it's very odd that somewhere in the process of our super entity, the motto on our very valuable currency would suddenly be changed from promoting the act of being an entrepreneur to promoting the act of being an employee or servant Basically from being a leader to being a follower.

Was there crisis brewing? Were there becoming too many bosses and not enough employees? Were there going be too many owners and those seeking to "mind their own business"? Once forced slave labor, which was mostly responsible for building this powerful entity was freed, thus reminding us of the constant benefits and rewards we receive from having faith and trusting in God, the leader of all leaders, with our well being, keeping us all in the mind state of being led and not leading? Shit!

They got me pondering again and I'm not trapping any cash! Like I said before, we are back to the basics. Understand the past to improve the future. I compare Mr. Franklin's statement while forging a nation, "mind your business" to President Obama's statement while restoring and rebuilding a nation, "we all need to step it up." There's a thin line between the two. Citizens are risking their lives in war, students are denied education, massive layoffs, recessions, no affordable health care, and everybody is hustling! The media manipulates so there's not mass hysteria, death, looting, robbery, murder, and suicide. America has peaked, the dollar is so inflated it's worthless and it's causing other institutions to crumble. Liberty is knocked down in the 12th round. One, two, three and there is no standing 8 count. We have got to mind our own damn business, step it the hell up. Stop playing and trap lots of cash.

Alfred Harvey

# CHAPTER 8

Alfred Harvey

## Section 1—Boom!! That's a Great Idea $

Ideas shape every part of our lives. Every day! You're going to have to excuse me, because this is hands down my freaking favorite! New ideas, new ideas,, new ideas! Yes, after I finish writing this I'll probably end up in a padded room, but who cares!

I love new ideas! To me, new ideas are like great music! And trust me, right now I'm really dancing! Like music, I'm so full of energy. As I write this, I turned the music up super loud while me and my dog are dancing from one end of the room to the other.

Yes, I celebrate everybody else's ideas and success, even if I didn't make a dime.

I just get excited and congratulate other people, I call it a boom! Our history is filled with free-minded Trap Stars who have changed a whole industry and or even our everyday boring lives. Boom! I love all of them from the tiniest post- it for doodling notes for quick thoughts that need to be remembered, boom! To the more technical ones that can level the playing field like the atomic bomb boom!

Wow! Do it again boom!

I love firecrackers but even more than anything, I love the art of the possible.

It's really amazing to create something new. There's no such thing as a bad idea, creation is always a great thing. I mean we all know there are some crazy ones out there, but good or bad is in the eye of the beholder. Who are we to judge?

I mean if I want a contraption that allows me to shoot olives into my martinis from across the room, then so be it, boom! Some inventors are famous, and some you may never even know. But who cares, a boom is a boom! I mean where would we be without peanut butter and jelly, boom!

Every one of us has a million dollar boom inside of us. We just have to find it.

Some people take their million-dollar idea to the grave with them because they never get the energy to pursue them. I think that's a total waste. If you have a great idea, which everyone does, and you know you're not going use it, give it away or sell it, duh! You can do what's called a poor man's patent where you write the idea's whole blueprint out and mail it to yourself and do not open it. The federal postage date can be used to dispute ownership of your idea. When it's opened up in court and the postmark is backdated.

People don't usually have to worry about someone stealing an idea. I mean it does happen, but not often. Most people have their own great ideas they haven't even pursued or showed up for and probably never will. But before you shop it around, a poor man's patent is a great way to start. There are other great places you can go with all the resources you will need to protect yourself, like U.S. Patent and Trademark office (USPTO): the website *www.uspto.gov* and United Inventors Association *www.uiausa.org* is a nonprofit company with lots of valuable resources. They have a yearly membership fee.

Last but not least, you know I love networking groups. Most big cities have groups for inventors but you have to show up. Check with the Economic Development Department or your local Chamber of Commerce. Boom! Feel free to contact me online. I will always direct you in the right direction and who knows? Maybe we can partner up.

Ideas are always transforming into big and tiny business ideas. So let's make a boom! You just have to think how the art of the possible has changed people's lives while making instant millionaires out of them and in some cases, maybe not millionaires but they are having no problem paying the bills, manufacturing something out of their garage that's locally a hot selling item, boom! You just have to use your heart and tinker a bit. Some things happen by accident, like the little kid who was breaking his toys while taking a bath and made a toy out of the broken toys that he wouldn't bathe without. Obviously one of his parents was an undercover trap star. Because the idea was taken to a major toy company and not only was the toy made, the kid was given a job as a tester and designer of toys. Boom! In the next section, I'll give you a few success stories to work with.

Alfred Harvey

## Section 2—I Make a Boom!!

I am really jamming. My IPod is filled with everything from Jay Z to Def Leppard.

Now there's a country song on called "Loving You is Fun." My heart has never smiled so hard. Baby loving you is fun." Ideas, ideas ideas! Boom! Gates boom! Jobs Boom! Walton Boom! I love it! Franklin boom! Edison boom! Ford boom! Dr. Dre boom! Cash Money boom!

Booms come in all shapes and sizes. For professional age confidentiality, I will withhold her name, but it's a phenomenal true story about a 14-year-old girl in Florida. Yes, you heard correctly, 14 years old and already a business owner. She was able to buy a home in default ("short sale") for around $12,000 from reselling other people's trash. Yes, you heard correct again, other people's trash. From what I hear, she's looking to buy another one and is collecting rent from people twice her age. That's what's up! Girl show up, boom! What about the Chicago based Trunk Club It's an online clothing spot for men. I'm wearing a sweat suit right now my wife purchased online from there. The service was launched in 2010 for guys like me who hate to shop or never seem to have time. They started with two employees and hit a million in sales the first year. Today it has over 100 employees and expects to reach $15 million plus in 2014. Good looking out for keeping ya boy fresh, boom!

Another great one is the Michigan company that patented and provides toilet paper with advertisements free to businesses to use in their public restrooms. Who knows, they may even add games next. StarToiletPaper.com, boom! I love success stories; I'm always the first to applaud a person for showing up and the last one to stop.

After Benjamin Franklin's great work started to spread, he was summoned to stand before the King. After his father, Josiah Franklin, had heard the good news, he sent Ben a letter quoting Solomon, "Seest thou a man diligent in his calling, he shall stand before kings he shall not stand before mere man." Boom! Google, boom! Facebook, boom! Twitter, boom! Michael Jackson, boom! Lennon, boom! Ozzy, Boom!

I'm still dancing! My excitement for idealist will never cease.

A moment of silence for those great people who have died while they were either in the process or after pushing all us humans forward as a whole (thank you so much)! Boom! Music's back on. I believe they would want us to dance for great ideas like basketball. Los Angeles Lakers, boom! Golf, boom! I know about a woman who, with her kids, slept in a car behind a carwash she worked at part time and later ended up owning it. Boom! I know of a drunken wino that hung around a liquor store from sunup to sundown and when the opportunity rose, he rose to the occasion and took over ownership, boom!

I have so many booms. Let's go back to the 1980's when IBM with their global size, dominated the world's personal computer industry. That was until a nineteen year old named Michael Dell, with $1,000 saved from a teenage stamp collection started a business that 13 years later would surpass IBM as the world's leading seller of personal computers. This caused IBM to exit the PC business and sell its operation to a company from China. How can a corporation worth billions be dominated by a teenager with pocket change? The teenager was willing to sell personal computers by mail and IBM thought it was too big to. Big mistake IBM, boom! Pet costumes, boom! Lunchables, boom! WWJD bracelets boom! I will see you in the next chapter. Got too hyped up and dove in the pool fully clothed. I think I ruined my phone (shaking my head). IPhone, boom!

Alfred Harvey

## Section 3—American Inventors Protection Act of 1999

Congress signed into law this protection act to protect American trap stars that create a new idea that can be patented including new processes, services or products.

I've been burned so many times by these firms that take advantage of people like you and me who just get so excited over our creations and get blinded. We turn into crazed mad scientists, "He's alive! He's alive!" There's nothing wrong with that, that's how we learn. I mean if the walls in my garage could talk (SMH). My wife and I stayed in the emergency rooms. I busted and banged myself up all the time and even partially severed a fingertip here and there. I've even fallen off the roof a few times. Alfred, what are you doing up there? Come down you're going hurt yourself. Oh my god mom, I can't watch this, Dad! It's okay, I got this, and sure enough, my big bang kaboom! Goofy sounds and I'm lying on the side of the house.

Thank God the city trash bins broke my fall. You know the ones I'm talking about the big blue and green ones.

I even caught myself on fire once from the chest up and had to be patted out by a friend. I had to get skin grafts on my arms and face for six months, boom! Put'em out! Put'em out! But that's all fine and dandy. The worst part is when you're swindled out of the money in your pocket because of invention firms. Now that hurts! "Congratulations!

Mr. Harvey, I'm the president of Invent Corp. Your idea was so good I wanted to contact you myself. I've reserved a whole team to move forward and patent and promote your idea. Do not talk to anyone about your idea because it's not fully protected yet. You will only have to cover your invention attorney retainer fees for your own protection.

After we receive this payment of a few thousands, we're ready to make you a millionaire.

Even my wife and kids gave me the thumbs up, anything to keep me off that damn roof (bless their hearts). But when it's all said and done, there never was an invention attorney, engineers, or development department. It's just some pill popping, drunk college dropout living in his parent's garage. Some keep getting fees out of you. Like congratulations, we got your patent! When you get it, you're running up and down the street showing off a fake patent certificate. You get the same reaction out of people who scratch a fake lottery ticket. There are a few stories of people who have told everybody off at work and walked off their job after receiving letters from well-known companies in Los Angeles or New York offering a decent amount of money once the development stage on your idea is complete.

My advice is, never rush, and never go in your pocket unless you have done a complete background check of the *invention development company* through the Attorney General or the Better Business Bureau. There is always a risk when you're asked to dig in your pockets. If your idea is that grand, your invention company would have no problem taking care of any fees needed to develop your idea. In the end you can be out all the money you put forward to develop your idea, not to mention the discouragement it will cause. So just protect yourself and take the time to do your homework.

## Section 4—Industry Developments

I really can't wait to see the improvements your ideas have on the different sectors in business. Just be sure to give my book a shout out when you change the game in manufacturing, retail, wholesaling, or the service industry because my word is my bond you will have my full support. I will constantly brag about your success and swag to inspire the next trap star coming up in the ranks, boom!

I have seen the tiniest ideas shift the whole crowd at a swap meet because a trap star found a sweet niche and the crowds are so large around their tables. It's like their new products are famous, signing autographs. We all have seen the effects Wal-Mart, K-Mart, and Target have had on the discount retail industry. In a time when consumer's wants and needs are changing, coupled with the recent technology explosion. Hungry starving trap stars are creating momentum trying to eat by any means necessary. Taking full advantage of what the larger corporations can't or won't do to respond to consumer trends. They're captive to their traditional ways of bigness.

The home business service industry is booming! Let me say that again, booming!

But go ahead and breathe, there's no rush. Just be humble and crawl in like a little ant and carry the whole building away on your back. Remember what I said about Dell boom!

## Section 5—Art of the Possible

Anything is possible, that's the whole art of it. Of course, nothing happens overnight. You will have to put some blood, sweat, and tears behind your idea and maybe even hang from the roof a few times. As long as you understand that the possibilities are always endless, that's not just a cliché that people like saying. It's been proven time and time again that they truly are endless. You are going have to believe in yourself first, and then against all odds, believe in your idea, know what it's capable of and have the passion to prove it to yourself. After you do that, the world will support your ingenuity and praise you for your cleverness to change or improve your way of life as well as mankind's.

The degree of usefulness isn't always the most important factor. Have you ever heard someone say, "I can't wait to see what he, or she comes up with next." A creator will always stand in an extraordinary league of their own, because they're not just curious dreamers; they have actually showed up and acted on their curiosity and wonder. Knowing it's not just about reaching their destination, but the overwhelming joy in each step they took to get there. Spectators can only marvel at the art of the possible. Where there's a will, there's a change.

Alfred Harvey

# Section 6—Humanity Got Rich Quick

The future is now! Finally, the little guy can compete and eat with the big boys.

In the last 0.01 percent of our history, 97 percent of all humanity's wealth was created. Those amazing figures are the equivalent to a nuclear explosion in growth of human wealth. Boom! It happened in such a very short period of time Humanity got rich quick. About the middle of the 1800's, the needle on humanity's prosperity graph shot straight up to another galaxy. The majority of the credit or cause of us trapping so much damn cash was the gathering in factories of power driven machines replacing the manual skills of laborers who produced goods from home.

The changes the transition from producing goods in house to the factory is known as the Industrial Revolution. During the same period, Adam Smith published his "Wealth of Nations" which was widely read. Adam Smith's book promoted the need for a more pro business policy. Government with less interference in business affairs.

I think I can, I think I can. The expansion of U.S. business was fueled by many inventions. Steamboats, boom! Telegraph, boom! Cotton gin, boom! Railroads, boom!

The banksters and their systems aided financially.

After the Civil War, the United States was experiencing some of the disadvantages of Laissez Faire, individual's freedom to pursue his own best interest without government regulation in a society that included very powerful individuals and big business.

Allowing individuals to pursue their best interests free from government regulation did not always serve the best interest of the country. I touch briefly on humanity's get rich quick scheme so you can understand the power of manufacturing one's ideas. There have been some grand changes in American manufacturing that you need to now because they're mind blowing. You won't want to miss this next explosion because it's happening now.

## HUMANITY GETS RICH QUICK

## 2.5 MILLION B.C. to 2000 A.D.

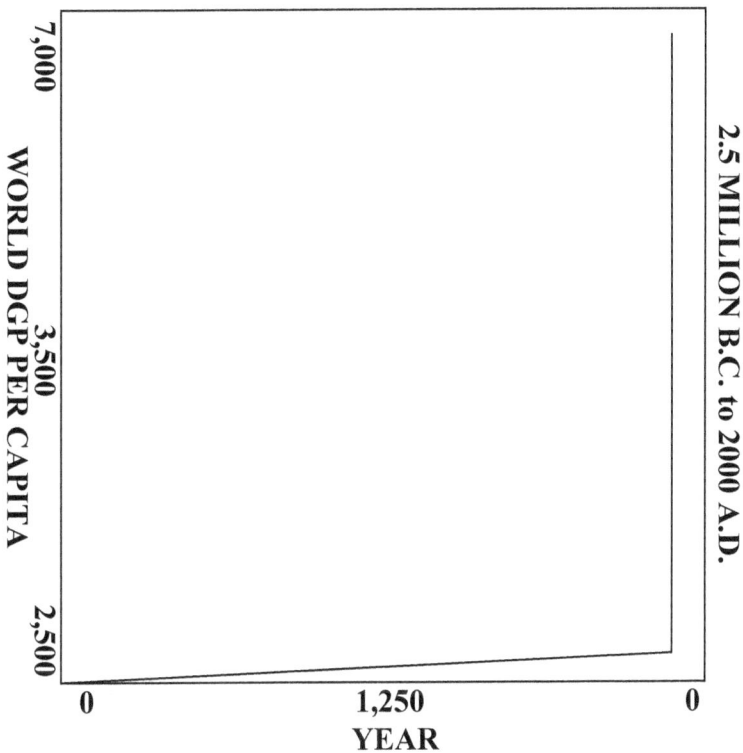

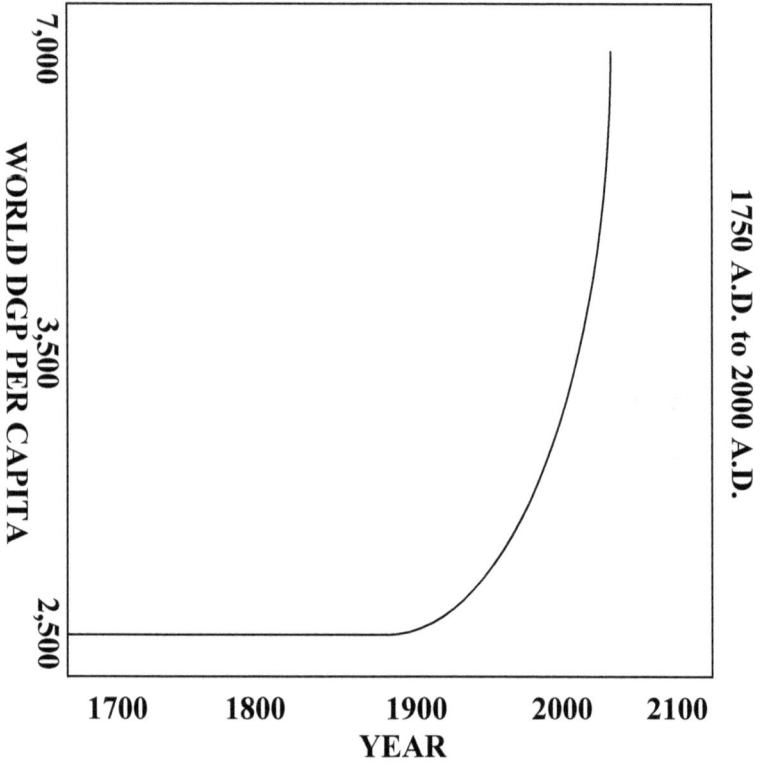

# Section 7—The Old Ways of Doing it Yourself Manufacturing

As you can see from the previous chapter, the possibilities of getting rich quicker and trapping mother lodes of cash are astronomical in the manufacturing realm.

One can't help but get excited, but I'm going hold my composure. It's just I already know about all the new changes that are happening in the world of manufacturing and now you will too. When I think about it, I just get stuck. I start to dream about all the possibilities and when I speak about them I get super pumped up and when I write about the changes, my hand just shakes.

With your brilliant idea, you will trap so much cash as well as conquer the world.

If your sights are just set on conquering your local area or neighborhood, well, that's really going be a nice walk in the park. Let me breathe a little bit and see if I can do this. Okay, let's do it! In the old days out of the four business sectors, retail, wholesale, service and manufacturing, it would usually cost the most to become a manufacturer of your ideas or even anyone else1s. It didn't matter about the potential for rewards.

Let's say you invented something new. Doesn't matter what it was. A hair-pick or a microphone and you wanted to manufacture it yourself. Well, in the past, you would have to find a location, buy the machines, tools, and equipment that you would need for production. You would make the dies, the drawing, pay your fees to the government authorities, determine your products best markets, make sales contracts, check credit ratings, advertise, promote your new product, buy all your supplies, materials and do some hiring of trusted employees. Are you broke yet? Most are at this point. You still have to pay transportation costs, begin distributing your product, and pay other running expenses like weekly payroll. All this is before you have made any money from your first sale. You would really be hoping that your product, once it starts to sell will cover all you have invested and start to trap some profits.

## Section 8—Based on a True Story

This story is about a man who while in his basement came up with a great idea for a windshield wiper motor and shopped his idea around to some major car companies.

One of them promised him a huge contract, so he decided to manufacture his idea.

He went all in with everything he had for his factory and then at the last minute, the major car company never made good on their promise of a huge contract. The man is up to his neck in loans and with no major contract, he defaulted and his creditors swarmed in to clean his assets out.

The man ended up on the streets and one day while walking in the rain, he spotted his idea on one of the newer model cars. To make a long story short, he ended up suing the car company, being awarded millions, but it took him a lifetime to get it. The man's story even inspired a movie. At the time, if there were a new industrial revolution going on like there is today, the man could have enjoyed all his deserved prosperity while he still had his youth and avoided all the unnecessary drama.

Alfred Harvey

# Section 9—New American Manufacturing is Here

The future is now. The Internet is a bad mammajama, let me tell you. With the democratize of many industries like communications, publishing, broadcasting and yes, manufacturing, not to mention many others, the traditional way of doing things has changed. The internet is making everything more socially equal in every aspect, including individual access to business and industry. It's making these huge traditional companies shift in their seat because our need for them is dwindling with a more 'do it yourself lifestyle growing and more people understanding it's more beneficial to the individual to retain more of their product's ownership in the long run than selling it out to a larger company. (Listen carefully this is very important stuff.)

Just a couple of years ago, a state of the art milling machine that you would need to produce your own idea or invention would have cost you around $150,000 plus.

I know none of us have that just lost under the cushions in our couches. The last time I checked mine; there was only a nickel, a dime, and a quarter under there.

I was searching everywhere for a dollar so I could get one of those great tasting corns with the mayo cheese and chili. This nice lady walks around the neighborhood selling until she sells all of them.

They're the bomb! She tells me she never has a problem selling out of them, boom!

The Chinese are changing the game and just copied all the state of the art milling machines. They just went from costing $150,000 to around $2,000 plus. I freaking love when they do that, boom! Now we can all have our own tiny factories in our garages making and inventing anything from can openers to clothes, jewelry, etc.

Go to buildyourowncnc.com, they have kits starting at around $1500. If you want something done right then you have to Do It *Yourself*. The D.I.Y. revolution in manufacturing is what you have been waiting for if you have the drive and are truly interested in trapping cash.

It can even be on the tiniest level. Imagine having a real cutesy idea for a hairbrush and being able to walk right out into your garage and simply make it ready to sell. OMG I'm getting excited. There's a great book you should check out called "Makers" by Cory Doctorow. It will put you even further in the loop with the scoop. Last year, handcrafting had sales in the billions. Just find your tiny niche and the sky is the limit, boom! I don't even need to tell you all the stories of instant millionaires who found theirs or made a great improvement on someone else's and the rest, as they say, was history.

You can handcraft woods, metals, plastics, and create anything you want like fine jewelry or even a chassis for a car. Just come up with something badass or simple like the Pet Rock or the Jumping Bean.

Just retire and play golf. You will just have to familiarize yourself with 3-D design software like Solid Works photo realistic rendering technology. Just snap a 3-D picture of an idea, add a few mind-blowing tweaks and the rendering technology and your milling machine will bring it to life right before your eyes.

The Shop bot PRS Alpha, which would run about $10,000, can work a wood piece the size of a door. Wow! New apps like replicator G, CNC laser cutters and lathes can make anything you want. Does it get any better than this? Yes! Let me tell you how. First, I have to thank a few for constant inspiration and proven techniques, ideas and support of this beautiful maker's revolution. Editor in chief Chris over at Wired, boom! Thanks man! American made by Martha Stewart (big kiss) boom! It was hard for me to embrace change from the street life, but people and companies like you have shown me a new direction. Red Bull, Boom! Virgin, Boom, I'm in space, boom!

Alfred Harvey

## Section 10—The Maker's Boom!

If you're like me and at times take doing it yourself to the extreme, you're constantly making booms that require the assistance of your local fire department, police, or emergency response teams. Then you will understand that my wife got really tired of almost having a heart attack, worrying about coming home to the pretty flashing blue and red police lights. Having to push through frowning neighbors to get to our house, because the whole block was evacuated due to a small explosion of some kind and I'm either unconscious or trapped under the house. Who could blame her, but me being accident prone, caused her to do a little research herself. What she discovered was, to me, worth millions. Thanks babe, I love you!

Let me show you the power of a nervous wife. With her very beautiful shaking hands, place the hugest padlock I have ever seen in my life, on the door of my tiny factory.

She jumped on Google with a vengeance and found out that you can do it yourself without having to do much of anything at all. I told you this was going to be good!

Let me explain. She found out that you could design and sell goods without any infrastructure or even inventory. Customize your ideas built to order and even mass produce with a virtual factory. Wow!

Thanks honey bunny cocoa beautiful me love you long time!

So when I continued her valuable research, Pandora's box was opened. I learned there are crowds of experts that will join your virtual factory and bring your ideas to life very simply. It's called open and crowd sourcing your ideas.

These clever "makers" are standing by waiting to help you. Just organize them and build. It even gets better. Yep! You heard me, follow me because the future is now. You can do any and everything in the virtual world. But some of us are not always quick to make the transition. Have no fear, now there are one-stop shops for manufacturing available in real life as well.

Let me give you an example. Kinko's is a great example for a one-stop shop, virtually and in real life, for printing and business needs, go online or even walk through their front door. Crowds of experts with access to all the top-notch equipment you will need to get the job you need done. What if I told you the same thing has happened in manufacturing? Would you believe me? Well, believe it. Thanks to the brilliant people like the founder of "Tech Shop," Jim Newton created a chain of workspaces where people like you and me can do it ourselves and have all the help we would need to manufacture our ideas. It's having your own factory without having your own factory. Go ahead Google Tech Shop, Menlo, California. It will blow your mind, boom!

# Section 11—How to Build Your Idea at Home

You're the trap star. Any garage can be your tiny factory and it's very simple and easy when it comes to limited production. It's digital not flammable, so have no fear. Here's how:

Step 1: <u>Invent</u>: come up with that great idea and check with the patent website and make sure it's not already patented by someone else.

Step 2: <u>Create</u>: There are so many free tools like Google's sketch up or Blender to design a 3-D digital model of your beautiful and valuable invention. Or just download someone else's great idea and improve on it. That happens all the time. You have the right to improve anything you want.

Step 3: <u>Prototype</u>: There are 3-D printers available for under $1,000 all you have to do is upload the file and watch the machine render your idea in layered ABS plastic.

Step 4: <u>Manufacturing</u>: Of course your garage is perfect, if you just want to conquer your local swap meet or retail stores, being the first to offer the amazing afro pick with the pistol grip. You will be able to make as many as you will need. But if you want to sell them to the rest of the world, factories in China are standing by and will connect you with the right people. Check out Alibaba.com, Boom!

Step 5: <u>Trap millions of dollars</u>: Sell and market your great idea directly to customers using the internet. There are stores like Ebay, Craigslist, Sparkfun, or you can use places like Yahoo or Web Studio and set up your online e-commerce. PayPal is even great, too. With this new age revolution, your idea will go straight into production with no financing or tooling required.

Trap University will not stop! We are committed to carrying valuable information by any means necessary. In support of change and making trapping, cash easier and possible to those unaware or otherwise not endowed with the opportunities. Who would, in the pursuit of happiness, sell themselves short and risk being locked up in American dungeons forever?

# EPILOGUE

Alfred Harvey

Hey ya'll, what's up? It's Alfred Harvey, aka "Zero". Yeah it's true when I started I was a good for nothing street hustler with zero dollars in my pockets. I remember it like it was yesterday, evicted by the U.S. Marshals, everything I owned in a couple of trash bags at my feet, tears in my eyes and soaking wet from the rain. "The only thing that counteracts "failure," in business, family, love and addiction is "failure." That rock bottom moment in your life will be the maker or breaker and determine the direction or path you will choose to travel on your way to success.

When you have zero dollars in your pockets all you will need is ambition. Define the word and then allow the definition to define you. I will be the first to tell you that I really didn't care too much for the statement, "If I could do it, then so can you," because everyone's situation is different. But whether I like the statement or not, in this situation, it's 100 percent true!

Failure gives you a keen eye and is one's true driving force. I am a well-known street hustler who for a long time embraced the whole gang culture, being shot, being stabbed, and a convicted felon who many times was alone in a cell. Extreme addiction not to mention I have even been hospitalized a few times, for mental issues due to the extremely painful contradictions in life, love and loyalty. I can compare my journey to a person trying to run from one side of the freeway to the other. At times, I'm still shaken. There's an old saying, "You can't beat an honest man." Why, because he's usually minding his own business and not yours.

At this point in my life, I am a full supporter of change. I believe all people are beautiful, every single soul on earth. I wish at times I could meet every last one of you. I know as individuals we must recognize our new beginnings and grab them for ourselves because nobody's going do it for us. The two things I have always had are "hustler's ambition" and a passion for business. Recently I have surfaced from the gutter and taken my place as a successful entrepreneur, businessman, consultant, author and most important of all, a father and husband.

When it comes to business, I like to think of myself as small-time and local. So I never forget where I come from or where I'm at. The street is where my love's at and it's where my love will stay. My passion for writing this book is to inform *those* who may not know that there are other easier and simpler ways to make money and succeed

Without God's grace and my business savvy, I know for a fact I wouldn't have made it to the other side of that freeway so many times in my past. I have personally founded ''Trap University'' to have an avenue to constantly bring you powerful, solid, proven techniques for trapping lots of cash that work! I have personally used these traps for many years to keep my family and me self-sufficient and out of the way…welcome to Trap University!

Alfred Harvey

# TRAP UNIVERSITY

Alfred Harvey

# CHAPTER ONE

Alfred Harvey

## Section 1—Benefits of Buying Cheap Land

Simply being able to pull your shotgun out on trespassers while you're still in your pajamas and saying "You need to get your little self off of my property right now or this is going be the last of you." Wow, imagine the joy in that! That's your land.

It's not your fault a couple of pot heads want to venture in to get a free taste of that top shelf, exclusive marijuana you're permitted by your state to cultivate. There are many benefits that stem from that little green, white, orange, or purple plant, so who can blame your trespassers? Well, from what I hear there's a lot of usage for the plant for medical purposes and recreational, relaxation, but who knows right.

The first and far most important things about buying cheap land is that it's yours! Acreage to most people seems so far out of reach, so they don't even think of it, but let me tell you, it's not. Most people are just not well informed, or they would jump on it. I mean who in their right mind wouldn't. I learned how to buy cheap land from a seventeen-year-old genius. He made a fortune throwing wild parties at a secret location in the mountains. He called them raves. For those of you who don't know, raves are huge hippie style summer of love parties and they're great! Well, from what I hear.

You can't tell that boy what he can't do with his land! You remember what happened at Waco? It wasn't Andrew's fault a few partygoers passed out from dehydration and had to be airlifted out.

Andrew bought his first parcel of land from the money he saved working at McDonalds.

At that time, he paid around $2500 for it. Yes, he made a fortune from his parties, but cleaned house when a growing renewable energy company came along and needed his land for solar power development. Today he's a proud owner of his very own McDonald's and is doing really well. I recently saw him at a gathering on some acreage of land that was purchased cheap on the outskirts of Big Bear, California. We're talking twenty plus acres for around $4,500, boom! Well, at the time, I just so happened to be in the area so I stopped by. Andrew and I laughed our asses off the whole night. I thought I was going have to be airlifted out.

Your land can be used for whatever you want, but I recommend you use it to do nothing other than trapping cash. There are many stories of people who have trapped a great deal of cash with land they bought for pennies. We all remember what Bugsy Siegel did with the cheap land he purchased in the Nevada desert. "Welcome to Las Vegas, what happens here stays here." That's a huge example just to show there's no limit. People are air lifted out of there every day and I don't see the government putting a stop to that anytime soon. Stay thirsty my friends!

Wal-Mart is another huge example of buying cheaper land on the outskirts of town and trapping lots of cash. The first Wal-Mart was opened in a rural area and later came to town with huge success. Now on a smaller scale, there are countless well-informed local stars trapping stupid amounts of cash in a number of ways, on the land they paid little or nothing for.

Alfred Harvey

## Section 2—Trap Cash Buying Land for Pennies

It is always a great time to buy cheap land. It's everywhere! Buying cheap acreage is always a sweet deal now and later. Yes, just like the candy we all have eaten, sweet! You can find it nationwide from California, Nevada, Arizona, or Texas and beyond down in the dirty south or back east. You just have to want it and start looking.

What if I told you that you could buy acres of land for what you would pay for a used car or that living room set you relax on and get nothing done? Well, believe it because it's true. It's possible to buy cheap land all over the United States; you just have to act on it. Most of us are always aspiring for world peace, but in the end when it just doesn't seem possible, we all have no problem settling for our very own piece of land. There's cheap land right under your noses, right where you live. The further you go out of town, the cheaper, and sweeter the deals will get. You can buy cheap land on the outskirts of town or deep into the wilderness. There's land for sale by private owners, realtors, banks, even the government. There's cheap farmland, industrial land, commercial land, all for sale and dirt-cheap. There's also land in remote and rural areas that is practically being given away. There are owners of an abundance of rolling hills that will have no problem giving you a great deal on acres of land.

I see up to ten acres of land being sold all the time for under $5,000. Yes, those numbers are correct! Five thousand or less! I promise you it won't drain your pockets like keeping that used car you bought running. It's actually the opposite. The land you buy can be used for trapping huge profits.

## Section 3—Different Ways to Trap Cash Buying Cheap Land

There are so many ways to trap cash with your newly purchased land; I really don't know where to start. I'm sure after I bring a few to your attention, you will come up with a few unique and ingenious ways to trap cash that are a better fit to your passion or expertise. I have seen people rent their land out for everything from farmer's markets, car shows, carnivals, small concerts, recreational vehicle parking (R.V.'s), festivals, or small vendor pow wows they organize selling everything under the sun (swap meets). People tend to come from great distances for great shows or deals.

Your land may be needed for a larger scheme for a huge company and they pay top dollar for the Deed to your land. You don't even need a brick structure. I've seen people trap huge profits under a large tent. The possibilities are truly unlimited. You give a young trap star like myself access to even an acre of land and trust me, I will find many different ways to fill everybody's pockets involved. Trust that!

I'm going let you in on a huge secret of mine that has been a proven moneymaker.

Property storage! This is very valuable information. You have seen these huge self-storage facilities all around town that store people's personal property for a monthly fee. We all know what happens if you default on your contract. You are locked out and your personal property is auctioned off to the highest bidder. Legally! So it's not just trapping cash on peoples need to store their precious property, there's a flip side - *industry*. When people are unable to pay for whatever reason, their units are sold for cash, privately and publicly, (storage wars). You already know I'm going give you the scoop on how to bid on storage units, how to place liens on stored property or even abandoned property and legally secure ownership in the later sections.

I just want to be the first to tell you that these huge public storage compounds aren't always needed. You just need to have, and you already know, land! The room to store people's cars, boats, RV's and any other property that may need to be stored. You can also be very competitive with fees, time limits on defaults and payment plans.

I've stored people's personal property in a two-car garage or anywhere else I could find to store it. I have trapped a pretty penny doing it. Let me tell you how to get your hands on this cheap land so you can do the same thing!

## Section 4—How to Buy Land Hella Cheap!!

Now that you know there is cheap land for sale and a few of the benefits owning it can have on your pockets, now I am going give you the strategies for buying cheap land. We have all witnessed the recent real estate crisis, sadly some even first hand.

We are all familiar with the condition of the economy, struggling during this recession. There are hidden benefits when an economy is on the verge of collapse. The value of real estate in many parts of the U.S. is at an all time low. Land, among other things, can be purchased cheap. Yes, you can buy land in some places for the price you paid for your television set. The choice is yours.

Now is a better time to buy than ever! Banks and the government have an abundance of foreclosed properties that land realtors and private land owners are desperate to sell. Whatever you do, don't believe them if they say they're not. Trust me they are desperate. It's ugly out here right now.

1. First things first. Land hunt, and know where you may want to buy. Like I said, there's cheap land for sale all over the United States. West, East, North and South right now. It will just take a little research and time to find, but I'm sure you can do it. Just familiarize yourself with what the land deals usually are in the area you're looking, so you

will know a deal when you see one. Depending on what you plan to do with your land, you may have to get a zoning permit. Unless you're thinking of throwing a secret hippie party, then you should have no problem with that. But then again, you can always disguise it as a cultural event and make a small donation to a cause or charity. With the technology today, water and electricity will never be a problem.

2.   The second thing you need to do is keep your eyes open. Talk to everyone. Show up at land auctions (public and private.) Yes, sometimes even uninvited. If you can't, by any means get into one then at least you can talk to the people leaving to see how they did. Bring some "I love land auctions" or ''got land'' t-shirts to sell. Everyone loves t-shirts. Just be sure you pick their brains. You're going have to look everywhere, like newspaper classifieds from any newspaper you can find. Network with groups on the internet. If I bought a piece of cheap land I would have no problem telling you where and for how much, unless I plan to go back and get the rest of it, but that's not always the case. Check out realtor.com, Ebay, craigslist and any other sites "cheap land for sale" brings you. Don't just check once, stay on it constantly. City hall will also have listings. Realtors have access to MLS, which is a standardized national system that allows them access, too many different listings on land and acreage for sale. So, just invite one over for some of your famous gumbo and you're in! Another few secret places to look on your next road trip are travel diners, truck stops, or signs on the side of the road. Remember,

talk to everyone. You may be able to find some cheap land for someone else to buy and both of you trap cash in the process.

3.   The third thing you will need to do besides keeping your eyes and ears wide open stay directly in contact with banks and the local government. Most of these institutions aren't in the business of buying and selling cheap land, so the land they do own is usually for sale dirt-cheap. Most are interested in selling quickly. They have acquired the land through foreclosures or by seizing the land, once the owners failed to pay on property taxes, or defaulted on a collateral loan, like a failed small business venture. Once again in the later chapters, I will explain how to buy government tax lien property. Trap University will always tell you how, and keep you well informed on the inside information to make it a lot easier for you to "stop playing and trap cash."

4.   The fourth thing you will need to do is search high and low, far and wide, for ordinary people selling their land, or just pieces of it. Working directly with the private sellers is where you can outwit the competition and find amazing deals. Remember, the economy is tough right now, so use that to your advantage. Post your own ads everywhere, stating you are interested in buying the cheapest land. I don't care if you say you're trying to start a reservation for stray cats. Just do what you must to get yourself in the cheap land for sale circles. Just a note to my readers: I am a full-blown animal owner and lover. No animals were harmed at any time in the process of me writing this

book or at any other time for that matter.

5.   The fifth thing you will need to do is have some kind of cash! That is unless you're asking for donations of cash or land for your animal retreat. Cash talks and the rest can't get cheap land. But always keep yourself open to everything. Google ''free land'' or "land giveaways". You never know. Making a cash offer when it's time to buy is very important. It doesn't matter what your offer is, make it. Throw offers out there even at times that you personally think nobody in their right mind would go for. Remember, you're the buyer, not the seller. You have to be tactful. Just for the fun of it, just walk in confident on land you may or not be interested in and say, "Listen, l'm ready to buy now. I'm willing to pay $200 per acre. Nothing more! Call me when you're ready!" Just be careful because the seller may counter and say, "Okay but you'll have to buy over 500 acres!" That's when you call me and everybody else you know so we can all get a piece of the action, unless that is if you can go the whole way on your own! I may only be in the market for 10 acres, but who knows what others may want. That is why networking is very important. Most land sellers would prefer the cash over a competing offer, which requires bank loan approvals or financing. The bottom line is there's cheap land everywhere. Grab some and use it to your advantage. It doesn't matter if it's acres in the middle of the desert! It will be yours.

Fraud Alert! There seems to be dishonest people everywhere with their hearts in the wrong places, always wanting to turn a positive into a negative. Let's not let them.

How we do this is by not letting go of our cash for those great land deals until we have checked with *The local county government*. Make sure the seller actually owns the land they are attempting to sell and the owners of the land aren't delinquent with liens pending against the property from creditors.

It's okay to jump on great deals, just don't jump off a cliff. These scam artists are very skillful, so just do your homework. I never recommend anyone buy land that you haven't seen. Who knows, your seller may fail to tell you that you're going need a boat or helicopter to access your newly purchased land.

Alfred Harvey

# CHAPTER 2

Alfred Harvey

## Section 1—Trapping Unlimited Cash with Abandoned Property

Abandoned property is a huge industry for trapping mega bucks. It's also a huge secret of success in the inner cities and usually left wide open on the outskirts of towns.

Anyone in your area who's trapping cash with abandoned property won't be quick to share or show you how the process works. Allow Trap University to be the first to fill you in on the process and the different ways anyone can trap cash with abandoned property.

Property abandonment is when its owner has abandoned a piece of property for whatever reason. There are many different reasons owners abandon property. Sometimes it's a crisis that is out of the owner's control, which causes the property to be abandoned, like death, being hospitalized, in some cases, even imprisonment. The most common cause usually stems from some sort of financial problem the owner of the property may be having at the time.

I've seen property abandoned out of pure stupidity and wastefulness as well, which gives birth to the saying, "One man's trash is another man's treasure." This statement is so true; you already see what the little 14-year-old girl did in Florida. Like I said in the earlier chapters of this book, she was able to buy houses cheap on "short sale" buying and selling other people's trash and abandoned property. You can use Google and get her whole inspiring story. Individuals don't always get the biggest award for being wasteful. The biggest award for being wasteful goes to companies in the public, as well as the private, sector. These companies throw out everything imaginable, everything from cars, equipment, computers, office supplies, even people! I will save that issue for another book. Right now, I want to teach you everything I know about trapping cash with abandoned property!

## Section 2—One Man's Trash is Another Man's Treasure

Let's take a moment and go back to that statement or title of this section because it's extremely important! I have been trapping cash for years taking advantage and legally securing ownership of abandoned property. By the time you are done reading this book you will have a greater understanding of the secrets and the many different ways you too can secure ownership of abandoned property.

Allow me to take you back about 20 years. I think I was around 15 years old. Abandoned on my good friend's parent's property was a dusty '86 Chevy El Camino Super Sport that looked really bad. The grass and weeds had grown up all around it. When I had asked my friends parents who it belonged to, their answer was, "We really don't know." They thought one of the tenants who had rented one of the back houses in the past had just left it when they moved out. The car had been there for as long as they could remember. They told me if I wanted it, I could have it.

I knew a thing or two about cars since I had already bought and sold a few around the neighborhood. I knew I needed more than just their word saying I could have the car to make the car mine. I needed legal ownership papers from the Department of Motor Vehicles. Who knew, the car could have been stolen! I also knew by having the VIN number ran, I would find out if the vehicle was stolen, or at least who was the last registered owner and their address. See, back in the day you had to have friends in high places to have a vehicle identification number (VIN) ran to get the goods on a car. Nowadays there are auto clearing services that will do it for free or you can go online to places like vehicle history.com and search preview free, or pay like a buck and get a full detailed report and vehicle history. It's that simple!

That goes for any piece of property with an identification number or in some cases a serial number. When my friend's parents gave me the Chevy, since I had a great love for cars, I hacked all the weeds down from around my new baby yelling, "Get away from her!" The whole time I did it, I had a friend running the vehicles identification number. I immediately, just for the fun of it, dropped her oil pan, flushed her radiator and gave her a major tune up. I even named her "Denise." When I fired her up for the first time, it was as if she roared, "I love you!" I love you too Denise! My friend came back with the information on my baby, the last owner's address and the fact that it wasn't reported stolen. It wouldn't have mattered anyway, because since it was abandoned on private property and I was given all rights to Denise from the owners of the land where her pretty self sat. I never moved her just legally started charging storage fees for the time she had been abandoned on my friend parent's property.

Instead of her last owner getting a letter stating, "Hey your car was abandoned, do you still want her? She runs great, just come on over and pick her up!" I knew I had to be slicker and slyer than that or risk losing Denise forever! So, instead of a letter just giving Denise back just that easy, I sent the last registered owner a lien sale notice attached to a certified letter stating that the vehicle had been abandoned on private property. The letter also stated that charges for storage of the vehicle had been accruing since the time of abandonment.

The storage fees being charged were the max permitted at that time by law. The lien sale notice also stated that the Department of Motor Vehicles had been notified about any and all debts owed against the title of the vehicle, which would prevent the sale of the vehicle in the future.

I also ran an ad in the local newspaper, which is required by law. By law, I had to post a notice of lien sale in a public paper, but the print on public notices are always printed so small no one ever pays any attention. The DMV (Department of Motor Vehicles) just wants proof of an effort being made to contact the registered owner to give them an opportunity. If they still have an interest in the vehicle, to pay all debts against the title or the vehicle will be sold in a lien sale to cover the storage, towing, and the price for the ad run in the public paper, to notify the public of the lien sale.

The registered owner has up to 45 days from the date the certified letter was sent out. By the time I was done the registered owners owed me approximately $2,700.00 for storage, towing and price of the ad I posted in the local newspaper. My whole out of pocket for the lien process and the ad I ran in the local paper, plus the certified letter was under $100. Of course, I'm not going count the work I did to tune Denise up. That was just a favor I did for her to help her through a rough patch she was going through in her life.

Denise's previous owner never answered the certified letter, so after the 45 days, I, the lien holder, received a letter from the Department of Motor Vehicles stating that Denise's title had been cleared and I, at any time during regular business hours, could come in and register myself as her new owner. You already know that's exactly what I did! Today Denise's estimated value is well over $10,000. No matter how that situation worked out with the $100 I spent on the lien process and the $150 tune up I gave her just for the hell of it, when and if her previous owner would have come to retrieve her, I would have still trapped $2,450 just from understanding and knowing how to take advantage of abandoned property. One man's trash is another man's treasure.

## Section 3—Clipboard Confidence

Abandoned property can be anything, like a car, bicycle, boat, power drill, washer, dryer, computer, a house, even land. Anything at all with or without an identification number that goes unclaimed is considered abandoned property. After I had my first taste of being the lien holder on a piece of abandoned property, you already know I didn't stop there! I went crazy once I realized I could legally secure ownership of the property in question.

A lien is the legal right to take the property of an owner as security or payment for a debt. The debt can be as small as a $40 charge paid to a local newspaper to run an ad attempting to find the owner of the abandoned property or a year's worth of storage charges accumulated over a period of time.

After securing ownership over my first piece of abandoned property, I ran wild and shot for the stars. I had clipboards I never used because they were for special occasions.

These weren't just brown wood and metal, these were my special ones! These were full of designs and color. I never used them because I always thought I had to fit a professional norm. That wasn't the case then because I was my own boss. I grabbed my purple and gold, yes my Laker clipboard, I was armed with all the confidence I needed to win.

I secured ownership of abandoned property everywhere! There were cars abandoned on the side of roads, on the freeway, in parking lots and garages, even on the side of people's houses or left on their land for long periods. I didn't just stop with cars. I secured ownership over boats, refrigerators, stoves, couches, bikes, recreation vehicles, and computers. It didn't matter what it was, I had a "move it or lose it" concept. If you left property behind when you were evicted or moved, I got the call. If a car was left in an unauthorized parking space for a long period, I got the call.

You already know I greased the palms of security guards, managers, landlords, neighbors, and business owners. I mean hey, I was cleaning up the city! No one wanted a dusty car on flat tires taking up space or any other property that looked abandoned or left behind. I quickly became the city's lost and found and abandoned property disposal unit. If the property went unclaimed, it was mine! In some cases, I would split the profits I trapped or give a percentage of the sale just to keep the calls rolling in.

Abandoned property is everywhere and it is not very hard to find. I will explain in the later sections how land and houses are even abandoned when the property taxes go unpaid. Yes, me the lien holder swoops in and becomes the new owner or just traps a profit in the process. "Move it or lose it."

## Section 4—Lien Mean Money Making Machine

When it comes to liens and abandoned property, different state's laws will vary. Laws we all must abide by. Some states are stricter than others. I must admit, the laws were put into place because of guys like me and our 'move it or lose it, pay now or later it's mine' attitudes. I mean you can call me shady if you want to, but business is business and we are all in it to do one thing, trap cash!

I, as well as the majority of thirsty business owners, operate under the business blocks that are the unbreakable structure our beautiful nation sits upon. You can't get any more patriotic than me. Hail free enterprise and capitalism! I will always capitalize when the opportunity arises and you should too. Always remember, this is the land of opportunity. This is what we do and we are the best at it!

Of course, I have legally secured ownership over other people's cars, trucks, boats, houses, and land on numerous occasions, among other things like motorcycles, recreational vehicles, and mobile homes. Everything from big screen TV's, to living room sets, computers, I think I even took a skateboard from a kid once. Hey, business is business. That skateboard was priced over $1,000 and the requested customization by the customer was even more. That's why you get everything in writing because when they can't pay, it's yours!

I really don't care what the property in question is worth, because to me, it becomes like a casino chip in Vegas that you just going throw away anyway. Who better to learn the abandoned property process from, than from a shrewd guy like me who will give you the real deal? I'm going show you the ropes to keep you off the ropes in the future.

We all know there's big money to be made in foreclosures when others default. You won't even have to defraud anyone. Trust me, there will always be those people who will fail to meet their obligations. People forfeit ownership everyday on everything for whatever reason. In the future, just by you knowing what to do when this happens, will always put you in a great position to trap cash.

# Section 5—Securing Ownership on Abandoned Property

There are many different ways you can legally secure ownership of abandoned property.

When you file a lien against a piece of property, you're basically saying that you are owed a debt, and before this property can be sold or claimed, you must be paid. The notice of lien sale has time constraints and if these time constraints that are set by law are not met, then the owner of the property risks losing it. It's considered property abandonment when you can't pay debts owed against your property within a timely manner. Once the lien process is started, the clock is ticking. Once your property has been sold to cover debts owed in a lien sale, it's gone!

People are legally taken advantage of every day, so much that there are groups that are trying to have the laws that are in place changed, because so many have lost their property. I mean no one likes to see the little old lady lose her home that's worth $250,000 because of $1200 in unpaid property taxes. The local government sells the lien against her property to a person who traps cash buying government property tax liens for pennies. Just so you know, it happens every day.

Property taxes must be paid or the government files a lien against the owner's property. Then to help the local economy, quickly sells the property tax liens to the public and if the property tax plus the interest isn't paid to the new lien holder within a timely manner, the lien holder has the legal right to secure ownership of the property. You already know, Trap University in the later chapters will explain more on how you can buy government property tax liens.

Right now I want to explain more about liens and abandoned property. When it comes to cars, boats and other property, it does no good to place a lien on property that the owner has abandoned without the intention of reclaiming. If the property has not been claimed within the time frame allotted by our state law, you can just conduct a lien sale for the property that has been abandoned: to be noted: Trap University does not at any time condone or promote unethical or immoral behavior, but will not hesitate to differ from standard textbook code, and let it be known it's a doggy dog world.

It's full of cutthroats who will use the laws that are in place to create loopholes that make taking advantage of unknowing property owners possible.

There are many cases where ownership has been secured legally on property that was never abandoned by the previous owner. They were just unaware of the proceedings and by the time it's brought to their attention, if ever, the charges for storage and/or towing have accumulated to the point that will actually cause the owner to hesitantly abandon their property due to lack of means or a momentary hardship of some kind.

People have taken possession of other people's property underhandedly with the intention to get cash out of the rightful owners for towing, storage, and the cost for the owners to be located. The owners can either pay, forfeit, or in some cases, have even gotten a judge involved to attempt to get the process reversed. But usually in the end, would cost a lot more money and with the judge's decision not always certain, leaves the rightful owners to weigh their options. The majority of the time, the owners will just pay or quit.

Sadly, there's a lot of room for scammers and their shady dealings. Under the disguise of a legitimate service to tow, store, or locate the property owners. They are protected by legislation and state laws on the way abandoned property should be handled. When you are ready to trap cash by operating an honest service with a reputation built on integrity, your community is ready and willing to embrace you as a pillar of decency. It doesn't matter who you are, your success will enjoy longevity.

With wealth and happiness, your cup will *overfloweth*. The shady route will always be short lived. Yeah, you may trap a few dollars but in the end, karma will always prevail. Positive energy will bring you the keys to the city and all green lights!

# Alfred Harvey

## Section 6—How to File Abandoned Property Liens

Who better to answer your questions when it comes to abandoned property and liens than me? I bring a lot of expertise to Trap University, and trust me, I'm not cheap!

I got over 20 years in the trenches. I have been in court on several occasions on both sides of the fence! I've legally secured ownership of abandoned property and at the same time have fought tooth and nail in front of a judge not to lose ownership of my own property. What they say is true, "What goes around comes around." Whether it's your customer, tenant, friend, or family member, it really doesn't matter who it is. If you do it yourself or just facilitate repairs, tows, or store property such as cars or boats and have not been paid by the owner of the property for services rendered, you are entitled to a lien against the property, vehicle, or vessel.

The liens become effective when the registered owner is presented with a written statement of the charges for your service. Always get everything in writing! However, if you take possession of property assisting a public agency or on private property at the request of the owners or management company, the lien becomes effective as soon as the vehicle is towed. "Possession is 9/10 of the law."

Research laws: First, you need to do research! Wherever the property has been abandoned, you are going want to know all the laws on how to legally handle abandoned property. Familiarize yourself with everything that is required by your state. It's just to protect yourself from being sued by an owner for *unlawful* disposal or damages. This doesn't happen often, but it's always better to be safe than sorry. Laws on abandoned property are usually loose. There are notice and time requirements you will need to follow. "No worries."

Locate: You want to be able to show you at least attempted to locate the owner of the property. Sending a certified letter to the owner's last known address is one of the great ways to show proof that you attempted to notify the owner of all current charges due, and fees that must be paid or their property rights will be terminated.

They will be denied access to their property and risk a lien if they don't pay in full by the set deadline.

Notice of lien sale: You have notified the owner of all charges or fees due and any deadlines, which may apply by sending an itemized statement by certified mail. Also, by certified mail, you will send a notice of lien sale, which will include all the information on the lien sale date, and any and all state law requirements.

Run an ad: When the lien sale notice deadline has expired, you must run an ad in a local public newspaper, where the lien sale will take place. You will have to check the guidelines within your state's law to see just how long your public notice will have to run.

<u>Going, going, sold!</u> When you conduct the abandoned property lien sale, your lien amount, and the cost of organizing or conducting the lien sale is cash trapped off the top! Just put that down in your shoe. Any extra cash trapped during the lien sale is to be held for the time required by your state law. The owner has the right to claim the balance by a set deadline. If not, then you might as well stop playing and trap that cash too.

What you need: the process for filing a lien on abandoned property is extremely easy.

You will only need the vehicle identification number (VIN). For motorcycles, you will need an engine number. For boats, you will need the hull number. If you lose possession of the vehicle that will immediately stop your lien. Moving or operating the vehicle is not allowed. In some cases, there's a large fine, not to mention it will also stop your lien.

You as the lien holder always have the right to pursue a court judgment to satisfy the lien. Any legal questions you may have, a lawyer will answer in minutes. Online, just go to sites like legalleinhelp.com and <u>law.justanswer.com/court</u>. They answer questions every nine minutes. There are also lien help experts and lien processing services that will handle the whole lien process for you at a low fee.

A ''short lien'' is for vehicles valued at less than $4,000 but more than

$500. A "long lien" is for vehicles valued at more than $4,000, or that is being stored at a storage facility. Vehicle short liens, long liens, even liens on boats, lien processors usually charge around $100 depending on whatever extra services will be needed. I strongly recommend you find a local lien processing company where you live and really get to know them. Trust me, you won't be sorry. (Hint, hint)

The different lien processing services I use on a constant basis all over southern California just shake their heads (private smile) when they see me coming. The things they are able to do for me when it comes to abandoned property liens and the overall process, I just don't feel they're charging enough, I mean I'm not complaining but every once in a while, when I can, I try and toss in a little extra. Thank you lien-processing companies! Boom!

You just take them the identification number for the car, boat, or motorcycle and make sure you have possession of the vehicle secured. They will take care of the rest.

They will also always know how to operate within the parameters of the law, keep everybody trapping cash and out of court. Trap on!

# CHAPTER 3

Alfred Harvey

## Section 1— Government Property Tax Liens

Government property tax liens are the bomb, boom! Whether people like it or not, you're able to secure ownership over property that's worth hundreds of thousands for pennies! Residential houses, commercial property, or even undeveloped land. As I said in the earlier sections, they're attempting to change the laws to make it impossible for me or anyone else to secure ownership of, let's say, a residential home worth $150,000 for $2200 in unpaid property tax. Let's just say this, those laws will not change!

It will always be possible to invest in a government property tax lien and secure ownership of the property, because when it comes to government property tax lien's they're backed by delinquent real estate. Boom! The laws won't change anytime soon because these cities and countries are fully dependent on property taxes being paid or they will go flat broke. Zero, no cash, lint, needy, poor, indigent, disrupted, full of obstacles, miserable, depressed, broken hearted, bankrupt, rough, ragged, crushed, looking funny, conquered, you know what broke is, I don't have to keep going! I know I do, "Daddy, I'm hungry! No daddy, I'm hungry right now! Broke!" To avoid this, the city, county, or local government stops playing and traps cash!

The government understands that unpaid property taxes are a form of property abandonment! So, in tax lien states, the local government created a loophole to trap cash by placing a tax lien. There's that word again "lien" boom! It places a lien on any property that the owner is offending by neglecting to pay their property taxes. The government gets delirious and takes a "You wanna play rough? Okay! Say hello to my lien friend!" attitude, then turns around and sells the lien to a guy like me, "Hi, I just really want your house and you out of it." I will trap cash on this one regardless. Either the owner can pay the owed property tax, or risk a lien and have to pay me interest because I bought the lien from the county to keep the local economy thriving. You already know that's a lie.

I invested in the lien the government placed on your property for the unpaid debt with hopes you're going through some sort of crisis or are just being mindless of your default, so I can come to your door and knock, when you answer I can say, "Get out!" If it just so happens to be the little old lady who loses her property just because she was careless and unguarded with her finances, (that's usually the face for the groups trying to lobby for change in the laws) well hey, "Ma'am, you're going have to pack your stuff up because this puppy is for sale. Have no worries because I'm going let you crash at my pad. My wife will stir-fry and you got my pad locked micro factory all to yourself. By the way, do you have any great ideas you have been wanting to pursue?"

## Section 2—Everybody Wins

Tax liens give the owner of the property a longer period to pay their property taxes.

So, by you investing in a tax lien, you're giving an owner more time to keep what's theirs. Just in case you're a *goodie two shoes,* and are having an attack of conscience about investing in a government tax lien, plus they're a very safe investment! Tax liens are regulated by the government and backed up by the real estate. There is going be no loss for the investor or the economy. Even the owner will get more time and we all know time is valuable.

Trap University must put you up on the fact that big property is being snatched by lien investors when owners default and can't pay their property tax. There's also always a flip side. If, or when, the owners pay their tax bill the lien investor just trapped lots of cash! There are many states you can invest in tax liens: Alabama, Arizona, Colorado, Florida, Illinois, Indiana, Iowa, Kentucky, Maryland, Mississippi, Missouri, Montana, Nebraska, New Jersey, New York, Nevada, South Carolina, Vermont, Washington D.C., West Virginia, Wyoming and wherever else they have adopted the process to stabilize their economy.

Alfred Harvey

## Section 3—How to Buy a Government Tax Lien

Counties sell lien property constantly, some more frequent than others. Some hold monthly auctions, payment is required within 2 days, so have your cash ready or already be financed to avoid delays.

The first thing you will want to do is know where you want to buy property. Local counties will have their own guidelines on tax lien sales.

The second thing you want to do is know what type of property you want. Do you want residential houses, commercial property, or land? Decide if you want an investment property for rental. The house is probably a great price but always factor in the needed repairs or you will spend more than you planned.

The third thing you want to do is network and research information about auctions all over the U.S.A. Your local county will post auction information and notices. Most of the time, they're within 30 days of the auction. Check the newspapers and local websites for any and all information. Go to sites like (your city) taxliensales.com or just taxliensales.com

The fourth thing is to set up the criteria of what you desire. For example, a specific zip code, the house must be less than eight years old, vacant, etc. Know how much cash is in your pocket so you can immediately know what tax liens are within your reach. When the bidding starts, you will have to know what's up with the property so you will have no problem spotting an inflated bid.

Last but not least, the fifth thing is bid! You can pre-bid in some counties. Just submit your bid before the auction gets started. Check with those in charge at the auctions to see if you must pre-register for the auction. Some auctions, you may be able to place online bids and not even be physically present. Imagine that!

Always consult an attorney locally to protect yourself from losing cash instead of trapping cash. There are also courses available, some online. You always want to continue sharpening your sword. If you visit ustaxassociation.com/free course, you can enroll today.

For the states that weren't named in this section, for instance, California, they may not call it government property tax lien investing. There is always something similar, but the process may just be slightly different. Don't be fooled, the majority of states will just foreclose the property themselves and sell the property for the debt owed on the unpaid property tax. You have to network, research, and analyze.

It starts in your neighborhood. It will be easier if you start right where you live, at least look into it. What do you have to lose? No loss, just gain!

# CHAPTER FOUR

# Section 1—Property Sells Short

As the real estate crisis boils over, our government officials and the elite banksters in our country, scurry about behind the scenes. Some even in public view pointing their fingers at each other about whose idea it was to dupe millions of Americans with these outrageous mortgage loans that were destined to fail. One thing's for sure, we have all become even more familiar with the term "foreclosure," and if not it's when they put you out of your home or kick you off your property legally! They sure did trap a lot of cash on that rap. Wow!

As I said in earlier sections, when debts are secured by liens against a piece of property and the property owner can't afford to pay the lien amounts in full, it's possible for the property to sell short of its value. *"Short Sale"* is when the proceeds from selling the property won't cover all the debts secured against the property by liens. The lien holder will have to release their lien on the property and accept less than what's owed. Creditors and the borrower will at times use a short sale as an alternative to foreclosure, because it's cheaper. It eases any added fees and costs for everybody involved. The property owner will still have a negative mark on their credit report, but the damage won't be as bad with a short sale as it would have been with a foreclosure.

Allow Trap University to be the first to tell you that creditors have become masters at processing these short sale applications because of this recent real estate crisis.

It's been hell for many people ever since this crisis unfolded in 2008. Short sales have become even more common. It's my job to bring the fact that they exist to your attention so you can take full advantage of securing ownership on property for cheap. In some cases, super cheap!

## Section 2—My Personal Experience

I personally try not to buy anything unless it's being sold short. It will always create, in the long run, a better advantage for trapping larger profits. I always network, befriend, charm even schmooze anyone I meet involved in real estate, like owners, agents, investors, brokers, also receptionists and office managers. I wouldn't care if it were the pizza delivery kid, we need to talk.

Talk to everyone. I talk to anyone that may be knowledgeable or even just overheard something I didn't that can possibly point me in the right direction or assist me in being able to buy a rental property for $7,000 that's worth about $90,000 at the peak of the housing market. (Oh my god I love you)!

I'm willing to do whatever it takes to close the deal or get the information I need (anything.) I've sent gifts like gift cards, concert or sports event tickets, shopping sprees, jewelry, cruise tickets, season passes to amusement parks, operas, free golf lessons even broken promises. Call it a bribe if you want to, bet you can't prove it! One time I got so engulfed in closing a deal I was unaware that my wife had noticed my receipts for the flowers and a piece of inexpensive jewelry I had delivered to a receptionist that worked for a large local real estate firm. This receptionist had all the inside information on a bunch of property that was going be sold on short sale and I wanted it!

I will be completely honest with you; this receptionist was innocent and a little naive. That didn't matter at all to me. I planned a fancy and elaborate dinner for the two of us so I could pick her brain completely.

She wasn't very committed to her company, because she was just giving me any and all the information I needed. There were many surprises she had to offer on a lot of local real estate deals. The more drinks she had, the looser she became. She was a treasure trove of information! The restaurant we were in was extremely trendy. There were even a few celebrities in attendance. The more I took the place in, I was in awe. I looked around and it was beautiful. I made a mental note to bring my wife when I got a chance.

Just then, I heard a glass break and heard what sounded like my name. The embarrassment caused me to shift in my seat like I was hearing things. "Alfred what the hell are you doing?" With a puzzled look on my face, I couldn't help but recognize my wife's beautiful voice. "Alfred, you heard me, what the hell are you doing here with this rachet? Who is she?" Realizing what was happening, I jumped up and said, "Honey, it's not what you think. This is a client." Just then, the receptionist spoke angrily saying, "I am not your client!" I couldn't believe I was caught up in this cheaters style scene, just without the security and the whole camera crew thing. Check please! We had the conversation on the importance of communication all the way to the house.

Before we arrived, she said, "That was a really nice place. Why haven't you ever taken me there?" Wow, what a night! In the weeks following, the receptionist brought a date and had dinner at our house. We were able to continue our conversation on real estate short sales. We all joined in the discussion when it came to great ideas for local businesses and the craziness of the restaurant incident. It was an enjoyable dinner, which ended with drinks by the pool. We all understood that we were in a better position now to trap lots of cash. Especially me! Boom!

Alfred Harvey

## Section 3—How to Buy a Short Sale

Trust me, whenever there's a short sale available, there's going be a trap star ready behind the scenes to grab it. The competition for a short sale can be ferocious with everybody and they mama trying to make an offer. By networking, you will better your chances of getting your hands on a short sale, sometimes way before they even make it on a sales list. That's the trick! You want to be well informed. Always ask questions like, are there any short sales popping? Do you have the inside scoop on the short sale? Here are a few ways to better your chances once you're ready to buy.

Act like a pro. Professional investors usually pay cash. Lenders know there's less risk when they see your guacamole up front. Always stay ready so you don't have to get ready. Befriending a few professional investors wouldn't hurt either. Just remember if you have one, always communicate any elaborate plans you may have for entertaining that new friend to your significant other (shaking my head.) If you're planning to use your credit, make sure all your payments have been made on time. Getting a pre-qualification plus letter will help your illusion of a minimized risk factor.

Second, put your money where your mouth is and make a strong offer. First time buyers usually put down an earnest cash deposit of about a grand. I've seen real estate contracts ask for that deposit to be placed in a trust account upon the approval of the short sale. If you put down around four percent of the sale price, you will put yourself well ahead of everyone else. The minimum down payment on FHA loans is 3.5 percent of the purchase price. Don't be afraid to turn into the *Hulk* and smash for what you want.

Be confident and very aggressive.

Thirdly, don't be duped or have your time wasted. Some short sales are priced super low just to attract buyers. Fewer than one in 10 short sales will close. Just because the home or property is listed at a short sale price, doesn't mean it's really for sale. You have to realize everybody wants to trap cash. To help you spot gimmicks, check comparable sales on realtor.com. Many banks will approve a short sale that is priced between 5 and 10 percent under market value. Always call your friends in high places to see if there are any other offers. Always ask what will need to be done to get your offer accepted and sent to the bank. Once that happens, everybody else is just wasting his or her time.

Fourth, don't jeopardize your deposit. Always have multiple inspectors ready to conduct your inspections. The majority of states standard purchase contracts give buyers up to 30 days to handle inspections without risking your deposit. Always keep a competitive edge or don't waste your time.

Fifth, pitch your tent and just chill. You have to communicate your willingness to be patient. I mean you are getting a great deal. You have to be willing to wait, sometimes up to four months. If your approval from the bank comes earlier, you have to be ready to jump with the reflexes of a cat. Your approval can come at around 3 weeks. Only the bank knows for sure. Most banks take around 8 weeks for approval. Just chill!

You're going be happy you waited. You would be surprised to know that many people walk away from many deals too early from not being patient and miss the deal of a lifetime. For the record, if by chance a short sale agent puts a lot of work in on your transaction and you just walk away from it like it's nothing, the next time you're most likely going have to find another agent. Be willing to relax.

Tip: Don't waste your time if your offer can't beat the competitors and still be below market.

Fraud alert: creditors are always suspected or accused of engaging in fraud during the short sale process. There are different types of fraud. One of the common ones is the creditor in the second position taking a pay off from the buyer and not disclosing it to the other creditors. Check out the "2010 CNBC Bank Fraud Story."

Patience, research, and determination. Let's not forget networking and you will always succeed. Short sale property is possible for everyone. Keep on trapping!

Alfred Harvey

# CHAPTER FIVE

# Section 1—Consignment Expert

I have been in resale for over 20 years. When it comes to resale, I am the man. I have been called everything from a natural, to a genius, the boss, even the best. There's practically nothing I haven't resold. When it comes to resale, I can't be beat. I won't be beat. It's literally impossible to beat me. I'm the master and the champion.

I'm too pretty to lose. You might as well call me the Muhammad Ali of resale. I am the greatest! If there were a shiny, sparkling, blinged out belt for the champion of resale, I would undoubtedly be wearing it. I've put more shopkeepers out of business than the freaking recession. If I open a store, yours is most likely going to close.

I had an attack of conscience once and closed one of my shops to allow an elderly retired couple a chance to thrive. I resale to trap cash, not for the fun of it. I have even ended up in court standing beside my lawyer a few times. Crazy, right?

I have been accused of the silliest things like operating without or an expired license.

Some counties want you to apply for a permit to resell used goods along with the required business license. I have been fined for loud music, neon lights, false advertisement,

"Sir that huge blinking neon light is going have to come down." City zoning violations will vary. "Sir I'm going need to see a permit for that elephant." One city tried to charge me with disturbing the peace and receiving and selling stolen property.

The funniest one to date has got to be when on one occasion a city cop gave me a sobriety test in front of my store, I failed it with flying colors and was arrested for public intoxication. My lawyer did a great job pleading to the judge. The fact was that I had walked to work and hadn't been drinking on the day of my arrest. I was just a little tipsy from the night before, oops! They will do anything to try to dethrone the king of resale. Some shopkeeper's best days in business have been on the days of my greatest blunders.

Karma is something else. I guess that's what I get for promoting the hugest "going out of business sale" and never truly going out of business. I will never go out of business, but everything else must go. Business is business, it's not personal. You have to understand the consignment concept. I have a duty to my customers to constantly bring them the greatest quality name brands at the lowest discounted prices. I also have a duty to my consigners to sell their items or property at a profit and a percentage of that profit going back into their pockets. It's not always the easiest thing to constantly create an "everybody wins" situation.

When you are the owner and operator of a consignment resell spot, shop or lot, the consigner is entrusting you, consignee with their property to sell up front and then give them the agreed upon percentage of the sale. They are providing you with some of their business inventory on consignment. It's really a sweet deal.

I have taken the smallest hole in the wall consignment shops and grown them into huge resell emporiums. As I said in the earlier chapters, I have been to the mountaintops. I started a used consignment car lot as a kid that had later become a full-blown car dealership. All with no out of pocket expense! Let me tell you how I do it.

Alfred Harvey

## Section 2—No Out of Pocket

There have been times when I haven't put any money at all up front, it's simple. I find a location that's been vacant for what seems like forever. Then negotiate what's called "Deferred rent" with the landlord. Deferred rent is when you don't owe rent, or it's postponed per the landlord while you build your business. The longest I have personally had my rent deferred was 9 months and that's long. If you need any longer than that then you should probably look into another business.

For a landlord to agree to defer your rent, they will have to be convinced of your vision or just respect your enthusiasm and not have anyone else competing for the vacant space. I have even negotiated my rent to be based off my businesses overall sales. "Sales based rent." The way this works is you make your books available to your landlord and they receive a percentage of the overall profit. These landlords are willing to try anything at times to fill spaces that are often vacant.

You just always keep throwing offers out there and if they bite then that's on them.

Alfred Harvey

## Section 3—Consignment Inventory

Before you even negotiate the lease on your space or buy that cheap land lot, you should already know the type of business you plan on operating. Let's say you're going to open a neighborhood market. You want to contact every vendor, supplier, grocer, butcher, and local dairy to see which ones will be willing to supply you on consignment. The local farms and dairies will usually have no problem supplying your market with all the eggs, milk, cheese, and fresh vegetables plus, whatever else they offer. If your market plans to have choice meats, then contact all the local butchers. Companies like Frito Lay and Pepsi Cola will have no problem supplying your store with all the snacks and beverages. Some companies will even send people out to your business free of charge to set up racks and displays promoting their company. As long as you have an account, they will have no problem replacing expired or outdated items and keeping you fresh 24 hours a day, 7 days a week.

This is why storeowners hate for you to walk in and just fill your pockets with merchandise. Everything has to be accounted and paid for. Once inventory has been completed, anything missing is considered a loss. Your loss!

Eventually not all your items being sold will be on consignment.

That's the point of buying and selling. You will be able to sooner or later buy at a wholesale price and sell at retail, or buy at a factory price and mark the price up. If you are on a land lot, you will not have a problem offering other people*s cars, boats, and RV's for sale or storage. Once you sell a car, everyone gets a percentage, so at some point the less you're selling on consignment, the better for your pockets. There's nothing wrong with using the consignment process as a crutch or brace for starting your business. Consignment inventory doesn't stop at cars or dairy products.

You can sell anyone's products or goods on consignment. Let's say you're going open a beauty supply store. Well, I would call every supplier or vendor around.

Locally or online and see which ones will supply your inventory on consignment.

It's just that simple. I've started a store once where the only item that I had to offer that wasn't consignment inventory was some lame designer T-shirts. They were the worst, but they were all I could afford at the time. My store still flourished and it wasn't long before the only item of consignment offered was some other local kids lame designer t-shirts.

A person's perseverance will always pay off in the end. There are many consignment shops that specialize in reselling clothes and accessories for younger kids and the little babies. They do very well with the right location and community buzz.

A lot of the time, people tend to get consignment shops confused with thrift stores, because they both resell used goods. Don't get me wrong, thrift stores can be a thriving investment, but usually are on the non-profit sector side when dealing with profit. Most of the inventory is locally donated and they usually are in support of a local cause or charity with all profits going back into the store. I bought a thrift store once in Hesperia California for a total of $3,200 complete. I flipped the business quick, selling it for $8,200 making a profit of $4,000. I just added a few hot selling consignment items for pets and added a hipster theme. No out of pocket; just some skilled decision-making. The neighborhood you will be operating in has a rhythm. Start out following that and you'll do fine.

Alfred Harvey

## Section 4—How to Open a Consignment Shop

You wouldn't be reading this book if you weren't really considering taking the leap into your own business and joining the resell industry. As I said earlier, I started out with a neighborhood used car resell lot. I later evolved and have resold everything from furniture, clothes, jewelry, and even food. I've sold consignment inventory at shops, lots, swaps, and spots with the ultimate goal and that's to trap cash. I am sharing my way and for me it has worked out Tony the Tiger Grrreat! Resell shops have always been the perfect place for me to sell everything!

Trap University is going give you the steps you need to follow to open your own resell shop. The best part is it will be yours. You make the rules; you can do it your way. Be your own boss, remember, there's no rules, just your rules. In your shop you can sell donated thrift items, consignment inventory, imported items from out of the country, designer this or designer that. Throw a party in the place if you choose. Don't waste your time playing, trap cash.

First thing you will need to do is pay your local city hall a visit and apply for a business license and a used goods resellers permit. Register your business name with the state. Be sure to grab a taxpayer's ID number. Always take the time to research any laws and guidelines you need to follow as a resell shop owner. At this point, you should already know what merchandise you plan to specialize in and sell. Remember you can always change the kind of merchandise you want to sell.

You make the rules. Always be willing to evolve.

The second thing you want to do is find a location and start building some conversation with the landlord. Location is always very important. You want your customers to have no problem accessing your store or finding a place to park. You can always share a space or get a booth at a swap meet. I'd take any space and make it do what it do. But that's me.

The third thing is inventory. You may think this is the hard part. Well, it's not.

It's simple. You will find merchandise by the boatloads. There are sales everywhere from yard sales to storage auctions. (I'm going explain in the later sections how to bid on storage units.) Plus you're going secure ownership of unlimited abandoned property. Consigners will always want their merchandise sold. There's always family, friends and neighbors. You will also have access to wholesalers and factory direct. There are ads galore online and in publications across the country.

The fourth thing you will want to do is throw your party. Yep, cut the ribbon.

Music, Bar-B-Que, invite the whole city. Potato salad, the famous gumbo,, special cheese. But go light on the wine. I had one grand opening go for a whole 2 days, wow! Make sure your merchandise is not a mess. Allow your customers to see your place is very well organized and clean. If you have the means, then throw a raffle for prizes. If your resale store is specialized for the kids, have a jumper, clown, candy, piñata etc. Use this time to really network your stores birthday. It's your choice if you want to donate any or all of your grand opening profits to a local charity or just help one family in need.

The fifth thing you want to do is, stay ready so you don't have to get ready. Have your consignment agreements ready and printed for your Grand Opening. Just in case, you have, customers wanting to sell item in your store right off the bat. Trust me, they're coming! Have your price tags and labels on your items and already have an idea of what you will charge to sell certain items. Everything is negotiable that's not marked 'firm'. "Ready, set, boom!"

The best part. Promote, promote, promote. Go crazy with your flyers and trump cards for business. Run an ad in your local paper, jump online and send emails, tags, and blogs. Even visit your local city websites and chat away. You already know what people are looking for, deals, bargains, and steals, so have a blast giving them what they want. "Yes, I would love to come to your grand opening. I am truly excited for you and I am your biggest fan." Earlier I said that I have been called 'the boss', but I have to put you up on a woman who is truly 'the boss' low key. She literally wrote the manual on everything you need to operate a successful resale shop. She's been doing it before I was born, wow! Take time to visit her website; http://www.TG+bt.com. She is truly an Icon of the resale industry and has helped me in so many ways. "Too good to be true." Thank you Auntie Kate, boom!

Let me say, I can't imagine life without a resell spot or lot. It's the greatest feeling in the world when you open your doors and start reselling everything under the sun. New, old, used or donated. This is your place. Do it your way, you're the boss. You are the greatest! By any means, "Stop playing and trap cash!"

# CHAPTER SIX

# Alfred Harvey

## Section 1—Abandoned Storage Auction Date

What better way for two people to start a relationship than with the possibilities of the both of them trapping a substantial amount of cash? I am by far a relationship guru, well, not yet anyway (wink)! You wouldn't be the first person to call me a lunatic who is badly in need of a hustler's anonymous group to regularly attend.

I wouldn't disagree with you on that one. I am very much aware of the fact that I am constantly mixing business with pleasure. As I said earlier, I don't stop my life to trap cash. I trap cash while I live life. Life is just a lot more enjoyable when you don't separate the two. You wouldn't have a life if it weren't for business, yet the first chance you get you try to ditch business so you can enjoy life.

You can never truly be complete if you don't combine business with the pleasures of your life. Most people are happier at home than when they are at work. Some people, even though most won't admit it, are happier at work and when they get home it's "Why I oughta"!

Whoever it was that made up *the don't mix business with pleasure rule* was not a trapstar. It had to be someone stuck in a dead end job that started a relationship with a dead beat at the job, and when it soured still had to see that person, while stuck in that dead end job. That's such a waste of time; I wouldn't wish that upon anyone.

Trap University is going make sure you're better prepared for the next time you're asked out to dinner and a movie. Now, dinner and a movie are fine, but should never be the first date. It just doesn't set the stage for a very healthy and prosperous relationship. Dinner and a movie on the first date are meaningless. It sets the stage for a life of sitting on the couch and watching TV Not very healthy.

The whole economy is upside down and more and more relationships fail because of financial reasons. Studies have shown financial hardship is the number one reason most relationships fail. This leads me to believe more relationships should start out with more meaningful dating, which has the possibility to uplift each other with a more entrepreneurial energy and fill the relationship with the spirit of business.

Relationships that are more new should start out with a more progressive attitude with the intent of moving forward powerfully. I'm just saying, who's going to cover for you or provide a distraction while you snatch a few "Hello, my name is" stickers off the desk and change the names to the two of yours, so you look like you were invited to this business conference. "Here, give 'em to me, let me do it, you're smearing the ink!" Who's going to give you that boost over the fence when you sneak into that private estate sale just to have a look around? "Baby, you can do this, just put your foot right here and there."

Two trapstars will always look as if you know someone. "Hey, I'm over here!" "Can you excuse me please, there he is." It's just being a team player and working well with others. Couples just have to get into a rhythm together and change the way they think about traditional dating and their futures as individuals as well as a pair.

Couples on those very important first dates will want to start frequenting seminars for business, entrepreneurial workshops even boot camps. Business invention conventions are the best. It's always great to enjoy a museum style conference with exhibit after exhibit set up with other people's new great ideas, and businesses breaking new ground, offering franchising options.

There are also wholesale and factory direct conventions and fairs offering products and goods for buying or selling, importing or exporting everything from art work, wine, clothes, jewelry toys and food. Who knew you could get $500 bottles of wine for $58 bucks a pop. Now you tell me you can't think of a way to trap some cash with that deal by the caseload. They also have name brand clothes and artwork.

Where else can you get $100 cigars for $5 a smoke and even cheaper, the more bulk you buy?

Those are just a few of my examples, but whatever your passions are, you will gravitate in that direction. It makes for a great date even if the couple has no intention of spending money. You can just go as curious spectators and watch what's going on in these places. People and product watching is always fun to a couple in their own little world. Just be careful because one of you or even both may just find a calling and see the opportunity to trap major cash. "Meeting you was fate, becoming your friend was a choice, but falling in love with you I had no control over."

## Section 2—She's Going to an Auction with Me!

Me and my wife's first date was at an abandoned storage unit auction. The way things worked out where out of my control. I had casually asked her would she consider going out with me on a date. She replied, "Sure"! When I asked her where she would like to go she replied, "It doesn't matter to me, I'm not very picky." So, being a trapstar, I decided I wouldn't break my normal schedule. I had plans to attend a local storage unit auction. So, I decided I would just include her into my plans.

She was a real open-minded person. I knew she liked home decor so I figured maybe she would enjoy herself, plus storage unit auctions have an abundance of home furnishings. People abandon their storage units every day and they're filled with personal property.

A person doesn't usually store something that doesn't have meaning to them. Storage units are, most of the time; jam packed from front to back. I go all the time; because it's a great place to come up on items, I can resell and trap cash. I have also kept things of great value and added them to my collection, like an engine out of a police cruiser that was still in great condition, a boat, gold, silver, and bronze items. There are a lot of collector items I go after like baseball cards, coins, stamps, even come up on collections of comic books, Star Wars toys and Garbage Pail Kids cards all in great condition. Maybe someday I will sell the stuff, maybe I won't, who knows. One thing I do know is I have trapped a lot of cash reselling everything families, businesses and the government have abandoned in these storage units, for whatever reason. Cars, boats, office supplies, home furnishings and personal property, there is everything you could ever imagine in these storage units being abandoned.

I buy everything and keep a special eye out for things I find of great value. I was really looking forward to our date. We already had great conversation and the flirting between us never ceased. I had already called and registered our names and an address, which is a requirement with most storage unit auctions. I won't lie to you, I was nervous that maybe she would think I was crazy to take her to an auction on our firstdate. She was already settled into a career she loved, so maybe she needed her dinner and a movie. I didn't know, I just took a risk.

"Sometimes in life you have to take risks."

## Section 3—Storage Auction Kisses

When I picked her up, she looked beautiful, like the prettiest flower I have ever seen. My stomach immediately twisted up in a knot. You know the feeling when you really like someone and their presence is overwhelming? When she jumped in my truck and pecked me on the lips with a kiss, I lost my train of thought. I said, "cigar twilights" and I meant to say, "There's a box of some really nice cigars under your seat. You can help yourself if you like. You can also watch a DVD, I have the whole "Twilight" saga and some others on demand."

Her reply was, "You can put the movie on if you want."

My nerves were on edge. I needed a martini! I couldn't believe the first thing I did was offer her a cigar (shaking my head.)

Whenever you go to a storage unit auction, you should always arrive early. We arrived at the storage facility, which was located on a hill that gave us a view of the city. I thought to myself, a little romantic. I was sweating! Since we were extremely early, I had to make a martini. I came prepared with a portable beverage bar. To my surprise she said, "Honey, you sit back. Let me make the drinks." Then she lit me one of those great tasting cigars. I was in heaven with an angel!

We enjoyed drinks while the movie was on. I explained how the bidding on storage units worked (as I will later in this chapter). We shared a lot of laughter and had the world in common. We ended up in an intense give and take discussion on sexology. It was a beautiful sunny day. We couldn't help but notice all the birds and bee's wings flapping and humming about. Life was crystal clear. We focused and watched while a flower was pollinated.

When auction time finally came, I had forgotten why we were even there. She was excited to see how the process worked. My initial plan was for us just to watch so I could explain while things were happening and why. She really got a kick out of how fast the auctioneers were able to talk. I bossed a few bids and won on some home furnishings she showed interest in. I didn't really care about the prices.

It was all in fun for me. I don't think I even spent a hundred bucks. All that mattered was we had a nice date. When I bought her lamps, she wouldn't stop kissing me. I thought to myself, wow, storage auction kisses!

The funniest thing that happened was when I received a message from her a few days later saying, "I had so much fun. We will have to do it again real soon and the online bid for those lamps we got is over $2,000 because they were part of an antique collection." I thought to myself, if she's selling them, then she owes me at least half. I made an illegal U-turn and headed straight for her place. I had all kinds of thoughts running through my head. "What did she know about antiques? She's a hair stylist! What does she know about online auctions? I don't even know about online auctions! I saw an opportunity to trap cash!

First, I would need her to sign some partnership paperwork so there would be no misunderstanding. I dialed her number and was shocked at her new voicemail. "Hello, you have reached Tee. I'm unavailable right now. I'm at another storage auction. I think I'm addicted. Leave a message!" I went off yelling, "How the hell can you put something I bought you up for sale?" I also told her about my half of the sale I felt I was entitled to. I barked about many things like the importance of honesty in a relationship. I admit she had me twisted and I was working with feelings. I needed to relax so I grabbed a bite to eat and went to see a movie.

It's so great to find that special person that wants to annoy you for the rest of your life.

I never got my half of the money for the lamps because she never sold them. It was just her way of finding out their value by how high the bid went. We frequented many more auctions and trapped lots of cash. Eventually we went half on a baby girl. I got the call from her stating that I needed to meet her over at the church on a certain date, wearing a white and teal green tuxedo, because there was some paperwork she needed me to sign. I walked down the aisle and was given away by my lawyer. I mean, I had to have him look over the paperwork and make sure everything was legally binding. It was a business doing pleasure with you.

## Section 4—How to Bid on Storage Units

While you're puffing that great tasting cigar and enjoying a modest 12 year old scotch, research all the local locations for self or public storage facilities in your area; the closer the better. You never know when you're going have to transport a whole house or office of abandoned merchandise. Check the yellow pages online, check with all the moving and storage companies you can find (talk to everyone).

Charm, schmooze, flirt, laugh, or crack jokes. Trap University has taught you well.

Know when to be serious and when to loosen up. There are resources. Search (your city) storage auction at http://www.location.com. There are chat rooms for self-storage and police auctions. Get all the locations. Who knows you may find one that's located on a hill with a view of the city. Calling and registering the names and addresses of those participating is usually required.

The second thing you want to do after you sober up enough from the scotch to legally drive or get a ride and stay thirsty. Your choice. Visit all the locations before the auction dates. I recommend you get a feel of the way auctions operate. Auctioneers are very fast talkers! If it's possible, try to preview everything prior to registering. Some auctions charge a non-refundable fee for registering to bid. Be very cautious of the auctioneers fast selling techniques. Better yet, just be completely sober.

I've been doing it for years so for me it's like shaving. Before you're ready, watch and learn. Always calculate your steps, and then bid.

The third thing we're going to need is your game face. Yes, ten toes down with your best look. You should be there super early like you slept in the parking lot the night before. You usually want to be an hour or so early so you have enough time to push your weight around like you own the place. Remember; full of confidence and in the greatest of spirits. Talk to everyone and go over all the details on units or items you may want to boss bid on. Register before bidding and revisit anything you may have missed on your first visit. Some items will still have their original warranties. Check the quoted price in the shopping guides when possible to ensure it's a great value. When you can, take a date who can prevent you from being too caught up in the bidding process and buying junk. (Why did you slap me?)

"No return" is usually the policy with most auctions. Everything is usually sold "as is." Even though that's the case, try not to use cash and pay using a credit card or check, because this will give you a way to return defective items.

Bidding on storage units can be very lucrative and fun. Always ask questions and stay up to date on storage unit auction laws for your protection. You're going trap cash and have a lot of fun. It's okay to be a spectator until you're ready.

"Keep on trapping."

Alfred Harvey

## Section 5—Abandoned Name Brand Clothes for Pennies

It's not always about what you know or who you know. Many times, it's about how you look! It doesn't matter if you have zero dollars in your pockets; you have to shine like new money. There are grooming standards! You have to dress to impress, "dress code strictly enforced." "You're going like the way you look, I guarantee it." You don't have to be brand new, just noticeably neat, sharp, sparkling more than not, crispy creased, so fresh and so clean. Your gear should always be snappy and so decisive and complete as to leave no loose ends or uncertainty. Thoroughly immaculate! You already know Trap University is going give you all the proven secret techniques only used by seasoned trap stars. It doesn't matter how much money you have in your pocket if you don't take advantage of a deal when it presents itself, then you're asleep and I'm about to wake you up.

I had just got off the Greyhound bus in New Orleans from Pomona, California and I had around $500 bucks in my pocket. That didn't matter to a trap star because I already knew by any means I wasn't leaving the Big Easy with less than $20,000 cash in my pocket going back to Cali. I had plans to take advantage of any and all the abandoned property that I could find, resell through consignment shops, lots and spots, always leaving my options open to the possibilities of facilitating the handshake between a buyer and seller on some cheap land for sale. I only traveled with one suitcase, which contained a couple of outfits, some cosmetics,and my portable office. I needed shelter, food, and some clothes so I could dress to impress and be clipboard confident, all on a budget. It didn't take much networking and I was able to locate Meyers Realtor off St. Charles, a nice older woman asked for my I.D. and $300 checked me into a modest clean European style studio apartment for a month.

My place was even located on the Mardi Gras parade route with a balcony view, boom!

Now for the grub.

I was starving and had heard way too much hype over the years about the food down there being the best and like no other. After shooting the breeze with a few really cool locals, I ended up at a place off Louisiana Ave.

Called, "The Brown Derby." Oh my god! The food will make you want to *slap yo mama.*

I was in awe when it came to the taste. The hype was true for around 7 bucks I was able to get a full serving of gumbo, greens on rice and a half a pound of hot and spicy crawfish. I sat on the curb to eat and the funniest little kid in the world, from the projects named Rodney was on his way to the French Quarter to tap dance tor tips using bottle caps he stuck to the bottom of his shoes. He had no problem taking time out of his busy day to stop and show me the proper way to crack the crawfish and said it was a must

I suck on the little heads to get the full effect. The food was the best I ever tasted to this day. Now with my belly on full and my taste buds satisfied, I needed the ultimate wardrobe and I already knew that getting it would be my easiest task.

My overconfidence comes from my positive energy and constantly succeeding in getting top-notch wardrobes on a budget. What happened next came with great surprise. It was Southern Hospitality at its best. First, just from asking around I found a shoe repair shop that was located in the French Quarter. When I walked in, the prettiest Creole woman I have ever seen greeted me. She was truly gorgeous!

I got straight to the point with her about how I was new in town and I had a last minute job offer at one of the local seafood eateries. I also stated to her that I thought the job would never call and that I really needed this job being new to the city and all. I went on to tell her that they were requiring black shoes that I didn't have and my money was tight. She immediately put her index finger up to her lips as if to say, "Say no more." Then she motioned me to follow her so I did just that. I went behind the counter and followed her down a hallway.

I was in awe and so grateful. We ended up in a small back room, where she pointed to three huge boxes of shoes and said, "You go through those boxes, and if you can find your size, whatever pair of shoes you want, you can have for $5.00." She then said, "I'll be back, take your time," and walked out with a pretty smile on her face.

I soon found out why she was smiling. When I looked in the boxes, it didn't take me long to realize I had hit the jackpot. People abandon shoes and clothes to shoe repair shops, dry cleaners, and consignment shops every day for whatever reason.

The merchandise is usually in excellent condition. These businesses have usually rendered services like dry cleaning, press with extra starch on a Tommy Hilfiger collar shirt, replaced buttons on a Dolce and Gabbana sports coat, or sewn a small rip in a Chanel blouse or sweater. Shoe repair shops repair zippers on leather coats from Wilsons to Gucci buckles on shoes. These services have all brands, styles, and accessories that are always being abandoned. You must know that they're not always quick to reveal they have garments they're willing to sell. They just don't want to develop a reputation for quickly selling their customer's garments or shoes when they're not picked up in a timely manner.

Once garments or shoes have been abandoned for what seems like forever and end up in boxes in the back of the store, they're just taking up space and "We have a business to run!" When I sat on the floor to try on shoes in the back of the shoe repair shop I was invited in, all the shoes looked brand spanking new or the shoe repair lady had skills!

All the leathers and suede I seen were polished and revived to brand new. I was able to find a pair of Gucci, Bally, and Kenneth Cole loafers. She even threw in a Hugo Boss belt for the hell of it. I got all that for $15.

The next place I went was a local dry cleaner and ran the same thing down to a nice older Asian man about my last minute job offer and how they were requiring a white collar shirt and black pants that I didn't have because my money was funny at the moment. I told him I would have no problem bringing my clothes to him for dry cleaning after I start working. He looked at me for a moment then said "Hold on." When he returned, he was wheeling two long racks, one with pants, the other with shirts. I quickly found everything I could fit. He charged me $3 a shirt and $5 for pants. When I left, I had five Ralph Lauren white button-down collar shirts from the Big Pony collection, three pair of Ralph Lauren jeans, two blue and one black. I also got a pair of Roberto Cavalli slacks all for $35, boom! I hit every shoe repair shop and dry cleaners in the downtown area as I do in every major city, in every state I travel to. I always have the same success. I have never been denied I was ready to stop playing and trap cash! Gucci down, all on a budget.

Alfred Harvey

## Section 6—You're the Expert

We all know that our economy right now is extremely chaotic. Everyone from the bottom to the top is feeling the pinch. At this point, we can't cry over spilled milk. We can just be grateful we got to eat the cereal. Now we all know that the milk after we eat that cereal is the best and anyone would be pissed off if they were prevented from drinking it. Just ask yourself, how many bowls of cereal have I had in the past and the milk was running down my chin?

As you're reading this book, just know your cup will overfloweth again. The abundance of life shall always return. Will you drink responsibly when it does is the question?

As you know, I asked, "will you?" because that's the only thing within your control.

You are the expert and self-control is the key to a full economic recovery. You have to lead by example and strengthen your position as a pillar of your community while constantly capitalizing on your strengths. That's how you show you care about the next man.

It doesn't matter if Mr. Economy is on Las Vegas Blvd., with milk running down his chin with his wife helping him into a limousine. You just act as the driver and get him home safely so Mr. Economy can have many brighter mornings. The way you do this is by training your eyes to see cash trapping opportunities. At the same time, minimize your spending and increase your savings while reducing your taxes. This will always put you in a better position no matter how hung over the economy is. You're the expert. Business is one big family. Yes, it's a family business!

Knowing this should make you dance up the street instead of walk. Everybody has a position; it's up to you to decide what you're planning to offer this family.

I will close with a brief prayer. "Father, please give them the angels they need to succeed and to love one another . . . amen. Hebrews 13:1-3: Let brotherly love continue (2) Do not forget to entertain strangers; for by doing so, some have unwittingly entertained angels. (3) Remember the prisoners as if chained with them. Those who are mistreated - since you yourselves are in the body also..." "In God we trust." Class dismissed!

"Trap cash don't let the cash trap you."

# ABOUT THE AUTHOR

Alfred "Zero" Harvey a well known street entrepreneur, businessman, author, and motivational speaker.

He grew up in the greater Los Angeles area in the city of Pomona, CA where he was first renowned as *"The Young Classified Ad Guru"* and an expert in buying, and selling by the Daily Report at the astounding age of twelve. He has always had a knack for business and a passion for creative writing.

Be sure to look for his upcoming titles such as *"My Babies Mama Works And I Don't"* The True Entrepreneurial Experience and *"M. Considerate"*, *"How To Succeed At Anything Using The Power Of*

# Alfred Harvey

*Consideration*" and "*Mama Said - Points To Ponder And Words Of Wisdom From Mothers Everywhere!!!*" And many, many more.